Generation X:
The Role of Culture on the Leadership Styles of Women in Leadership Positions

Dr. Remi Alapo

ASTA
PUBLICATIONS

Printed in the United States of America

DEDICATED

To all Generation X women in leadership positions.

To Chief Mrs. Olabisi Olateru-Olagbegi,
Executive Director, Women's Consortium of Nigeria (WOCON).
"Aunty Bisi", you surely will be missed.

ACKNOWLEDGEMENTS

Almighty God for allowing me the opportunity to complete my doctoral studies in a timely manner. Thank you, Lord, for letting me have the vision to conduct a research dedicated to my years of being a woman in a leadership position. I am grateful that I am able to publish the results of my dissertation into a book with practical explanations on organizational challenges and some ways in which women in general and those in the Generation X age group in particular can self-identify their leadership styles and understand better how to lead others in different organizational settings.

My family both far and near, especially my parents Dr. and Mrs. Alapo. My father Timothy Gbadegesin whom I credit for where I got my hard work from. I have not known any other person who is very energetic and stays up all night to ensure that work is done diligently. My mother, Madam Christiana Kofoworola, who has been my number one cheerleader from the very beginning. I thank you for encouraging me to always go for the best and never to settle for less. May you continue to enjoy the fruits of your labor. My brothers and sisters: Abioye (and his family), Yemisi, Adeola (and her husband Mr. Femi Osewa), Shola, Lola and Yinka—thank you for all the support and for believing in me. My Uncle John Alapo. My nephews and nieces Emmanuel "Akande," Joshua "Joshy," Faith "Faithy,"—Aunty Remi's Baby, and Daniel "Danny-Tippy"— I love you.

Members of the African Women's Caucus of the UN Commission on the Status of Women (CSW). Members of the NGO Committee on the United Nations International Decade of The World's Indigenous Peoples. Women's Consortium of Nigeria (WOCON), for allowing me to serve as a United Nations representative for the organization on women, human rights, sustainable development, and on human trafficking issues. Cora Weiss and my former colleagues on the NGO Working Group on Women, Peace, and Security—UNSC Res. 1325. I am eternally grateful to you for allowing me the opportunity to collaborate with you. Thank you for exposing me to the work, plight, and activism of women around the world. I have learned a lot from the various groups and communities over the last 15 years.

My University of Phoenix Cohort members—it was a pleasure meeting and learning with you all. Mrs. Ini Onuk, thank you for providing assistance during my data collection by linking me with members of WIMBIZ organization (Women in Business) in Lagos, Nigeria. Mr. Roberto Castaneda Sarabia, thank you for providing the data analysis and additional feedback for my oral defense. It was a pleasure working with you from Mexico. The women's auxiliary of the Ahmadiyya Muslim Community Center of New York. Women's Federation for World Peace (WFWP) Metro New York Chapter - Thank you Mrs. Beryl Green, chapter chairwoman for creating a community of sisterhood and support. Women's Press Collective (WPC), for providing grassroots women's organizations working on gender justice a safe place to advance with the publication of their work. National Coalition of Concerned Legal Professionals -(Kathleen at the NYC Office). Dr. Ada Okika, Mr. Wale Ajibade, Amb. Caroline Usikpedo, Mr. Gbenga Omotayo, Dr. Michael Akintayo and Mr. Alain Tchegnon–Thank you all for the support and invitation to continue research and work together on gender justice with civil society organizations.

Dr. Rolf D. Schlunze, co-head of SIEM, Japan (Spaces of International Economy and Management), for allowing me the opportunity to co-present a session on Management Geography at the AAG conferences in 2012. David Rockefeller —Thank you for everything. Assuanta Howard at ASTA Publications, for being very efficient in getting the corrected versions to me as promptly as possible. It has been a pleasure working with you.

Finally, to all my colleagues, friends and well-wishers—especially my research participants, and everyone that came to the initial book launch event, thank you for your support and interest in women's rights for equality and advancement. As the saying goes, "'The sky is

the limit' and 'Aluta continua, victoria acerta!' The struggle contin-
ues!"

In solidarity,

Dr. Remi Alapo

TABLE OF CONTENTS

INTRODUCTION

The 21st century has been met with increases in integrating cultures and economies at a faster pace (Suk-Hing Chan, 2005). The global economy demands national cultures to adjust to global market trends. To understand the wide scale of global and multi-national business practices and international environments, national and organizational leaders are forced to step out of the norms of their country's national cultures and leadership practices (Suk-Hing Chan & Oueini, 2005). As the world integrates businesses and cultures, organizational leaders are crossed between their cultural beliefs and practices. Many are also confronting a myriad of leadership approaches in order to understand the cultural influences on leadership (House, Hanges et al., 1999).

Generation X: The Role of Culture on the Leadership Styles of Women in Leadership Positions addresses some of the factors that have contributed to the need for organizational leaders in adjusting to the globalization of the workforce, the expansion of international companies, and the exposure of many national organizations to increased business competition. Increased competition has forced organizational leaders to deal with the cultural limitations of particular organizational and leadership practices. Additionally, researchers in the 21st century have posited that culture is a condition and boundary to previous leadership theories and practices (Hanges, Lord et al., 2000).

The study of power as part of an organizational political action by all stakeholders is an emerging field of interest aimed at improving individual leadership and organizational effectiveness. The definition of power is a person's capacity to persuade another person to do something. Income, social class, political influence, and property can determine a person's ability to hold a position of power in society (Thio, 1992). All participants within a group possess power.

They use power regardless of organization type, gender, rank, and social class. Men and women emphasize different ways to manipulate power, as do subordinates compared to superiors and peers. The political dynamics of groups become dependent on the presence of power and its use.

The focus group selected for this book is the Generation X age group of women in leadership positions. The group involved an organization's body of members, characterized by their unique culture, values, and social beliefs.

Generation X: The Role of Culture on the Leadership Styles of Women in Leadership Positions' goal is to assist organizational leaders to view Generation X women in positions of power from a different perspective. Women leaders are capable of leading a 21st century organization because of their scope in knowledge about growing businesses, and their ability to blend and incorporate new technologies and innovations in the business environment (Alapo, 2013). "Innovation is the specific function of entrepreneurship, whether in an existing business, a public service institution, or a new venture started by a lone individual in the family kitchen. It is the means by which the entrepreneur either creates new wealth-producing resources or endows existing resources with enhanced potential for creating wealth" (Drucker, 2002, p.4).

This book also serves as a model for inter-cultural or multi-cultural business organizations, in which diverse women from different ethnic, educational, religious, social, and economic backgrounds are capable of using their opportunities as women in leadership positions to encourage and mentor younger generations of women in attaining leadership positions.

Generation X:
The Role of Culture on the
Leadership Styles of
Women in Leadership Positions

CHAPTER ONE

BASES OF POWER

Organizational power politics permeates all actions within an organization. Power is one person's ability to exert change on another person's way of life and actions (Sweeney & McFarlin, 2002). Using power is a valuable means to influence and achieve intended desires and future action in others. Power is instrumental; it is a way to achieve goals (other than the attainment of power itself).

Power has utility for the group members most often as an intermediary tool to achieve some personal desired end value (Palumbo, 1969). There are several reasons to obtain power, including the following: (a) to achieve a goal, (b) to reward supporters or followers, (c) to deter opponents, (d) to coerce subordinates into performing certain actions, (d) to gain expert knowledge, and (e) to gain ideas over others (McShane & Travaglione, 2003). Throughout history, the theory of power has been depicted in various organizational settings, nobles or elites having more power in society over commoners and those with less wealth, men holding certain positions over women, and so on. The works of Karl Marx describes how those with money have certain influences over those who do not have money or wealth.

Marx's Theory of Capitalism, the Elite theories, and the Pluralist theories are used to measure power and the formation of inequalities in gender roles (Christian & Howson, 2009). The works of Karl Marx in the 19th century and Max Weber in the 20th century showed that Elitist theories, such as social class and economic structure, sometimes determine the ways in which leaders use power (Christian & Howson, 2009). According to pluralist theories, members' success in a group or in an organization is dependent on the appropriateness of the particular power tactics or leadership styles used in person's political dynamics with others in a specific group (Christian, 2008).

Marxist's theories of power state that a person can hold power as a result of economic and political influence in the society, and not necessarily because he or she holds an elected office or is in a position of power within an organization (Christian & Howson, 2009).

Social psychologists French and Raven (1960) identified five bases of power that have laid the groundwork for most discussions on power and authority in the latter half of the twentieth century. These five types of power are coercive, legitimate, reward, referent, and expert. Power can be manifested through one or more of these bases.

Organizations attempting to streamline their operations for maximum efficiency may implement a coercive power method (Victor & Turner, 2006). Employees who are often coerced have more on-the-job dissatisfaction, lack commitment to the organization, and experience withdrawal from their job's and organization's goals. Overall, coercing employees leads to a decline in their ability to be productive, a fact that often affects the bottom line of organizations.

Provided below are brief descriptions of four types of power that conceptualizes how a person may or may not be influenced by power in an organizational setting.

Reward power is a positive power that refers to the ability to get work done through others by one's power to grant rewards. Such rewards could be either tangible or intangible rewards. For example, a leader or manager can reward employees with money, a flexible schedule, or a job promotion as a way of acknowledging their positive contributions to the success of the organization.

Legitimate power depends on organizational position and authority. This type of power refers to that which is conferred by a person's organizational position or acknowledgment as an authority figure in an organization. This type of power is based on the premise that an organizational leader has the authority and the right to give orders based on their position within the organization. While employees may comply with legitimate power based on the authority or role of a leader, it does not mean that they will be cooperative in an organizational setting or commit to prescribed goals set by the leadership within an organization (Victor & Turner, 2006).

Expert power derives from a person's expertise or specialized knowledge of a certain subject. For example, a person may specialize in a specific task within an organization who do not possess the same knowledge or skill. They become "experts" in the knowledge they possess over others and not necessarily because they are superior in class to others within the same organizational structure. Another example is that a manager may have more knowledge or skills than his or her subordinates with the same years of experience on the job, but the manager has expert knowledge over their subordinates because he or she may have acquired further knowledge of how to perform a specific task within an organization.

Referent power refers to the power that comes from people identifying with an individual and attempting to emulate that individual's behavior. The person who acts as a model for reference has power over the person who emulates his behavior because obviously the person being emulated acts as a role model or possesses some expertise or positive influence within the organization or in the society. An example of this would be found in a transformational leadership approach, in which a leader can move along their subordinates with charismatic behavior. Some people tend to admire leaders in specific industries or organizations who have impacted their lives both directly and indirectly, irrespective of their social, philanthropic or financial contributions to society or specific organizations. This emulation of a person's contributions to society is known as referent power because the person is seen as a transformational leader, able to carry people along positively. How a person identifies with a person as a reference is shown differently in different cross-cultural contexts.

In cross-cultural environments, French and Raven (1960) have point-ed out the ways in which subordinates relate to those in authority. Many cultures use different meanings, symbols, and gestures when interacting with those in authority. For example, interactions with Asian and specifically Japanese managers is that subordinates most often will not look at those in positions of power directly in the face. This is also similar to many African cultures where those in posi-tions of authority are held in high esteem and subordinates and have a fear of authority when interacting with their supervisors, managers or those in positions of power. Therefore, referent power is primarily based on trust, particularly for employees who are unaware that they are emulating their leader or those in positions of authority.

Power in an organizational setting can sustain goals and lead to cen-tral authority among subordinates, followers, or peers (Kleiner & Sable, 2007). Power can prove discretion on an organization's prog-ress or culture; it can also increase the value and visibility of a leader within and outside of the organizational setting (McShane & Trava-glione, 2003). Four factors serve best to determine behavior within a firm: personalities, stage of organizational development, scarce resources, and ambiguous circumstances. These factors also dictate group politics within an organization (Mastenbroek, 2005).

The consequences of a leader with power in an organizational set-ting can bring about commitment, approval, compliance, or resis-tance from others; and the results he achieves reflect the ability of that leader to exercise good leadership within the organization (Noll, 2001). The use of power can also mean using explicit or implicit be-haviors that are assigned to an individual or prohibited to lead oth-ers in leadership positions (Sweeney & McFarlin, 2002). A leader's capacity to handle and manipulate the different forms of power will directly have an effect on his or her leadership in an organization.

However, to better understand a leader and his or her use of power, we must first understand what a leader is. Leadership is defined as the ability to influence the decisions, opinions, attitudes, and behaviors of others using some sort of power in an organizational setting (Choi, 2004). Leadership can also be described as the way in which a leader interacts with his or her followers to achieve a common or set goal (Darity, 2008 & Lee, 2001). With leadership qualities–which can be thoughts, feelings, or visible behavior—a person can lead an organization with power either through coercion, aggressiveness, persuasion politeness, or by inspiring others in an organizational setting (Ashraf, n.d). A leader's behavior becomes a key factor in designating interactions with group members.

According to Bass (1990), the make-up of a leader is a combination of natural phenomenon, as he or she is affected by the environment, in addition to the desire to attain such a post. A person may also carry out a formal study to acquire necessary leadership skills. Leaders are to understand others even when they function outside of a leaders' set of demographics. Personality traits and events that happen in people's lives in their environments, coupled with the willingness to become a leader and study necessary skills, are all approaches to becoming a leader.

Leaders should understand subordinates' needs through fostering trust and communication, and assisting followers to understand and make relevant the goals and values of the organization (Bolman & Deal, 2003). Within the organization, a leader's performance and interaction with the team will influence the ways in which his or her leadership styles reduce or eliminate opposition (Cherniss & Goleman, 2001).

Additionally, a person's cultural values and setting play a significant role in the portrayal and usage of power to influence others (Scott, 2003). Many societies interpret power as control or the ability to influence policy or decision making. Culture remains a powerful subliminal influence because the effects of culture on individual behavior are lasting. Over time, culture determines collective behavior as well as group perception, values, and thought patterns (Schein (1999). Societal cultures also dictate whether a person's leadership style is either positive or negative depending on environmental factors present in a society, which can be shaped by a person's values, norms and beliefs.

To better understand some of the different dimensions of power that leads to how and why organizational leaders relate to subordinates or why certain people interact differently within an organization in a specific way, the works of Hofstede were used as examples in the study. There are other studies on cross –cultural leadership that have been conducted such as those by the GLOBE organization (acronym for Global Leadership and Organizational Behavior Effectiveness), the cross-cultural research effort which conducted studies believed to have exceeded the results of other cross–cultural leadership studies (including Hofstede's landmark 1980 study–used as the reference in this publication's cross-cultural leadership section) in scope, depth, duration, and sophistication (House et al., 2004).

Hofstede's work is relevant and better suited for this research purpose in providing a general understanding for the basis of cross-cultural leadership and the way in which those in positions of power relate to their subordinates and how subordinates can understand themselves within the general culture of an organization. A brief description is provided below before for readers to understand better in basic terms and definition, the dimensions to leadership.

Hofstede (1980, 1991, 1994, 2001) developed a cultural dimension model based on a research study done in 67 countries. In the study, Hofstede discussed the influence of culture on individual behavior. Hofstede identified four dimensions:

1. **Power distance.** This cultural element describes the degree of inequality among people who are considered acceptable.

2. **Individualism/collectivism.** Individualism implies a loosely knit social framework in which people take care of themselves and

their immediate families only, whereas collectivism characterizes a tight social framework in which people distinguish between in-groups and out-groups.

3. **Masculinity/femininity.** This aspect focuses on the degree to which values and traits in society are associated with masculine qualities.

4. **Uncertainty avoidance.** This element describes the extent to which a society can deal with threatening, ambiguous, or anxiety-provoking situations.

5. *Long-term/short-term orientation.* A culture's orientation reflects whether members of the culture accept delayed rewards and gratification or not.

CHAPTER TWO

HISTORICAL PERSPECTIVES ON WOMEN AND LEADERSHIP IN NIGERIA

This chapter identifies in brief the chronological and historical factors relating to the leadership of women in Nigeria from the pre-colonial, colonial, post-colonial, and present-day Nigeria. The historical and chronological differences in leadership and perspectives of Nigerian women during these periods as well as the demographic and leadership characteristics that may have contributed to the growth or decline of women's leadership are discussed (Bradely, 2005).

Women in Pre-Colonial Nigeria

Women in pre-colonial Nigeria, depending on which ethnic group they belonged to, had prescribed and assigned roles within the Nigerian society (Akiyode-Afolabi & Arogundade, 2003; Okome, 2002). With these prescribed and assigned roles, many women groups in pre-colonial Nigeria sometimes were able to form support groups that assisted women in the society with leadership roles, especially those within the immediate community (Adu, 2008; Okome, 2002). Before the year 1900, the dynamics of culture and the influence of women's ability to occupy leadership positions using different forms of power tactics varied from one society to another (Rojas, 1994).

In southern Nigeria, for instance, there were no formal separate and explicit political institutions and roles (Atanda, 1973 & Babayemi, 1974). Historically, women occupied many ranks and commanded various roles within the palace and community administrations. The Igala tradition of the middle belt region of Northern Nigeria served to prove the ranking of women without boundaries to gender, but much acknowledgment of a person's capacity to perform; history holds that a woman, Ebele Ejaunu, founded the Igala kingdom.

Northern Nigeria was the home of prominent women sovereigns and women of power such as Queen Amina of Zaria in the fifteenth century, who extended her influence to the Nupe Kingdom, built many cities in Northern Nigeria, and was a skilled merchant credited with introducing kola nut to the region (Lebeuf, 1963/94a).

In other societies, culture and class dictated sex differentiation that resulted in women forming strong organizations. Examples of such organizations were seen among the Igbo and Ibibio people of South-East and Eastern Nigeria respectively where women were very much independent and had control of their day-to-day activities on the basis of their collective political and economic strength (Yusuf-Raji, 1998). In instances in which female political and economic organization were lacking, such as among the Efik, Edo, Itsekiri, Ijaw, and Kalabari ethnic groups in Southern Nigeria, women of high status exercised political power as a collective representative of other women in the society through the office of the queen mother of Benin and through his or her personal relationships with the male rulers (Pearce, 2001).

Pre-colonial African institutions were not formerly designed to model European institutions but to maximize on individual capabilities that were put to the service of an entire nation. The absence of European-type institutions did not declare the absence of order in pre-colonial Africa, where humans were ranked according to complementary skills for the survival of an entire nation. The leadership role of the pre-colonial African woman was valued as a necessary complementary factor rather than a subordinate position subservient to the men of that era.

Women in Colonial Nigeria

During the colonial era, many women groups' activities were suppressed because of colonial policies and structures that undermined the already existing cultures and societal groups. These policies eliminated many support structures that existed for women's groups

(Adu, 2008; Akiyode-Afolabi & Arogundade, 2003; Okome, 2002). The colonial economy oriented in export, undermining the prestige of the traditional occupations of Nigerian women. Colonial policies and statutes were clearly sexist and biased against women occupying roles in leadership and economic positions (Okome, n.d). European Colonialists stripped the Nigerian women of all leadership positions and power. The Colonialists debased the ranking of Nigerian women to fall below that of European men and women, European youths of all ages, and finally Nigerian men of all statuses (Rojas, 1994).

Despite the obvious efforts from European colonialists, Nigerian women remained persistent in the quest to excerpt and manipulate power. Women in Eastern Nigeria beginning in 1929 resisted foreign invasion (Effah Attoe, n.d). They combined the struggle for independence with attempts to re-dress the socio-economic policies of the colonial administration by staging the 'Aba Women's Boycott' that was a collective political strategy to question colonial authorities on economic grounds and show the damaging impact of colonizers socio-economic policies on women's lives. In Western Nigeria, under the leadership of Ransome-Kuti, women questioned the character of the authoritarian governance and the arbitrary nature of decision-making by the colonial governments. The women were strategic in their approach and used power tactics such as threatening to walk naked to the Oba's palace in Abeokuta. This was a sign that traditionally, women owned the power and authority of decision-making to question authorities in unfair social, political, and economic practices.

Women in Post-Colonial Nigeria

Post–colonial Nigeria adopted numerous policies of the colonial era, which resulted in undermined and limited roles of women in leadership positions (Bah, 2004; Okome, 2000). Many of these biased policies significantly reduced women's social, economic, and political power, especially in the areas of leadership and decision-making (Akiyode-Afolabi & Arogundade, 2003). Nigerian women insisted on maintaining their pre-colonial status in post-colonial Nigeria. Women carried a systematic struggle to regain power influence and to maintain a voice in the relationship between state and citizens and a voice in the relationship among the people (Oduaran & Okukpon, 1997).

The plight of Nigerian women for inclusion in the political, social and economic affairs is still ongoing. There have been significant improvements regarding women and leadership but for the purpose of this book and not to deviate from the research, brief assertions are made regarding women's leadership in Nigeria since the second case study was conducted there. Women cannot be denied their leadership roles as negotiators on equality platforms, especially those in the focus group for this book—the Generation X woman (Pearce, 2001). The baby boomer generation brings a different perspective into economics and politics, based on experience and difference in gender dimension that asserts itself on the political and economic scene rooted on traditional frameworks based on ethnicity, religion, age, values, and class.

Women and Leadership in Nigeria

Women in Nigeria continue to face enormous setbacks regarding development and leadership capabilities (Igunboh, 2005; Manuh, 1998; & Okome, 2000). The socio and economic roles that many women occupy in Nigerian society affect leadership roles, especially in the context of the sexual division of labor and in decision-making (Igunboh, 2005; Okome, 2002; & Osiruemu, 2004). Challenged by the progress made by women globally, Nigerian women currently engage in the struggle and advocacy for political and economic inclusion. Through various coalitions and efforts, Affirmative Action, CEDAW, and Gender and Constitution, women have been addressing the issues of political marginalization and key leadership and decision making capacities.

The progress of Nigerian women is one challenged by the very nature of such progress; women in leadership positions are sometimes known to assert more transactional and autocratic styles because they are excelling to prove themselves to their male competitors. Despite their escalation in ranks in the Nigerian society, many women in leadership positions are still bound by national and family culture-assigned roles and duties. A new generation, however, is emerging faster than the baby boomers. These are the Generation X women, who are much more independent and have their own businesses, and lead in many 21st century organizations.

CHAPTER THREE

LEADERSHIP AND DECISION-MAKING STYLES

According to Dubois (2006), "Leadership is the process whereby one individual influences other group members toward the attainment of defined group or organizational goals" (p. 62). Evans (1996) suggested that leadership philosophy is conceptualized as the leader's values, behavior, and attitudes. Fuchs and Hofkirchner (2005) also suggested examining gender differences in the characteristics of executive leaders regarding management styles, strategic behavior, work-related values, family, and work conflict.

Pro-social outcomes of relationship competence and transformational leadership are mediated by the development of empathy, collaborative approaches to conflict, self-disclosure, and social interest (Jogulu & Wood, 2006). Gallivan (2004) determined communication styles are predetermined by societies. A secure sense of awareness develops positive models for engaging in exploration and risk-taking. Frize (2005) proposed that a self-efficacy process could have a positive impact on individuals before they choose to initiate their efforts. Similarly, Jogulu and Wood believed people have a tendency to weigh, evaluate, and integrate information about their perceived capabilities before they make decisions.

Autocratic Leadership

The autocratic leader is also referred to as an authoritarian leader. According to Bass (1990), autocratic leaders do not communicate with the employees beyond what is minimally required; they prefer definitive structures and dictate commands that followers are expected to comply. Authoritarian leaders do not welcome input from followers and are not concerned with followers' personal well-being (Likert, 1967). The despotic rulers of history preferred this type of leadership. The impact of an autocratic leader results in independent and submissive followers who act more productive in the presence of the leader and less productive when the leader is absent (Argyris, 1953; Lewin, 1948; Lippitt & White, 1957).

Today, the autocratic style is not the preferred leadership approach because it does not encompass social dynamics and the building of relationships within a group. However, some organizations exist in which practicing this leadership style is necessary to achieve positive results (Marques, 2006).

While some believe that the autocratic style of leadership should never be practiced, Dew illustrated how this type of leadership can be an advantage within the right context. When leaders exert auto-cratic behaviors, it may serve to avoid conflict in instances where employees are submissive, but it may also create resentment and re-sistance against leadership and management. Another downside is that it may also lead to a fight for control between employees and management (Dew, 1995). Rotemberg and Saloner (1993) believed the autocratic style of leadership can be useful when the organiza-tional environment lacks new ideas.

Democratic Leadership

This book uses Tierney's (1989) definition of organizational democ-racy. Tierney (1989) stated "… democracy concerns the manner in which organizational participants define and come to terms with the principles of social justice, equality, diversity, and empowerment" (p. 125). The democratic leader is someone who prefers to establish direction based upon the opinions of the majority. Marques (2006) described the democratic style of leadership as beneficial within the academic environment when implemented.

Dew described conflict resolution within an environment led by a democratic leader. "Democratic leaders come to understand that conflict is a normal part of any team effort. Each individual has a different type of personality, different knowledge, and different experiences. It is perfectly normal for people to be in conflict. Democratic leadership allows conflicts over issues and personalities to be resolved instead of denied. Conflict over control tends to disappear" (Dew, 1995, p. 53).

Laissez-Faire Leadership

Lewin, Lippitt, and White (1939) conducted a study to examine leadership within boys' clubs that resulted in one of the first references of the laissez-faire leadership style. The study determined that autocratic leaders demonstrated more control over the laissez-faire leaders. Laissez-faire leaders adhere to the status quo and rarely interfere or cause conflict by introducing new strategies or organizational direction.

In the laissez-faire style, the leader has a more standoff approach to leading and allows subordinates to manage themselves. This approach works best in organizations that have a strong sense of self-direction and highly skilled workers who can manage their customers (Marques, 2006). The productivity, satisfaction, and cohesion of organizations led by laissez-faire leaders are hindered by leaders who are unable to provide sound direction (Bass, 1990).

Transformational Leadership

Transformational leadership is significant because of its application to current work situations (Avolio, Bhatia, Koh, & Zhu, 2004; Beng-Chong & Ployhart, 2004). Beng-Chong and Ployhart posited that since changes within the economy affect organizations, leaders of organizations must contend with uncertainties in market fluctuation. A transformational leader must be able to view the organization as constantly reinvented to implement change when needed for improvement (Sashkin,1988).

An organization should be reviewed from a level that permits the vision and the future of the organization to be interpreted, with appropriate goals, objectives, and strategic plans clearly set (Burns, 1978; McCabe & Naude, 2005; Russell & Tucker, 2004).

Women generally display transformational leadership traits. A study by Groves (2005) discovered that women's extraordinary social and emotional competencies assist in appealing leadership behaviors. Given the powerful effects of charismatic leadership on team cohesion, organizational performance, and follower performance and attitudes, women may indeed possess a decided advantage regarding the interpersonal skills and behaviors necessary for effective leadership in modern, change-oriented organizations (Groves, 2005, p. 40). Atwater, Avolio, and Bass (1996) found that men are more likely to display transactional leadership than women, while women tend to perform transformational leadership behaviors, particularly individualized consideration, more often than men.

In opposition, Komives (1991) and Maher (1997) found that transformational leadership is not influenced by gender. Carless (1998) and Gazso (2004) found that superiors rated female managers higher on transformational leadership while their subordinates rated men and women equally on transformational leadership style.

In contrast, men exceeded women on the transactional scales of management-by-exception and laissez-faire leadership. The results of these studies are inconsistent, but they do suggest that women score slightly higher on transformational leadership style assessments than men.

The transformational leadership style encourages subordinates more than other leadership styles, which tend to be more authoritative. The results of using transformational leadership are caring employers and loyal and lasting employees who will remain faithful to the organization (Archambeau, 2006).

Today, women are occupying leadership roles traditionally occupied by men. As transformational leadership theory becomes more popular with organizations (Morrissey & Schmidt, 2008), the relationship between gender and leadership style has been an increasing topic of interest to organizations (Catalyst, 2005). The studies indicating a higher rating for women on the transformational scales are significant for the future of women executives (Morrissey & Schmidt, 2008). The increase of research results that point to a positive relationship between organizational success and transformational leadership is in contrast to results that indicate a negative relationship between management-by-exception passive leadership and laissez-faire leadership (Thyer, 2004).

The investigation of why women score higher than men on levels of transformational leadership has launched several theories. One theory is that women have to meet higher standards than men to attain and retain leadership roles. Another theory states that women in management meet with resistance when they demonstrate traditional authoritative styles. Proponents of this theory believe that women leaders' gender roles in society are similar to a transformational leadership style in management (Backhouse, Burns, Dani, & Masood, 2006).

Decision-Making Styles

The leadership skills necessary for management are rooted in good judgment and decision-making; these leadership skills also lead to wisdom. One can measure a leader's wisdom by the way in which he or she appropriates judgment and decision making to the right situation. According to Kennerly and McGuire (2006), wisdom is an action-oriented construct. Many organizational decisions are highly complex. Due to the intricate nature of some decisions, a broad knowledge base facilitates understanding, interpreting, and integrating the information for better decisions or outcomes.

Kedia, Nordtvedt, and Perez (2002) posited that uncertainty is the sole reason organizational leaders search for additional relevant information to find clarity. Leaders acquire additional information by scanning the environment for useful data and synthesizing all information for better decisions (Kedia et al.). To acquire the skills necessary to maintain a competing enterprise, decision-makers need to immerse themselves in the current flow of information and real time engagements, which will in turn lead to improved personal skills and knowledge in these respective skills. Eiserhardt (as cited in Kedia et al.) discovered no major differences for why leaders sought additional information when he wrote, "When decision-makers immerse themselves in real-time information, they acquire deep personal knowledge of the enterprise" (p. 26). The argument supports the contingency theory, which urges leaders to consider more than one source of information in the decision-making process.

No universally accepted classification of decision-making styles exists, and decision makers differ with respect to the information used, the alternatives considered, and the integration of multiple inputs (Bradberry, Eberlin, Kottraba, & Tatum, 2005). The fundamental consideration should not be just the decision-making style, but also the type of decision reached. Rausch (2005) and Bradberry et al. agreed that leaders should distinguish that effective actions are the foundation of sound decisions, and sound decisions originate from understanding of all controllable matters that could affect the result.

Women in leadership and decision-making roles can influence the policies and directions of organizations (Ahuja, 2002). Ahuja posited that women in leadership value support from their organizations. In contrast, Catalyst (2005) described the negative stereotypes and perceptions of women in leadership positions and their abilities may be a factor for gender disparity in decision-making amongst men and women in many organizations. For an organization to flourish, leaders need to act selflessly and put organization's needs before their own. One of the downfalls to the success of an organization is the shortage of dedicated qualified talents who are willing to make the necessary personal adjustments to bring forth success.

CHAPTER FOUR

THEORETICAL PERSPECTIVES OF LEADERSHIP

It is clear, even within the same culture or society, that all leaders lead organizations differently because multiple leadership styles exist. Which style a leader chooses is often based on cultural values, beliefs, and norms (Marcoulides, 1995). These leadership styles are directly and indirectly influenced by societal messages of tolerance, either subliminal or present.

An evolution over many years has created leadership theories and leadership styles, such as the great man theory, trait theory, contingency theory, path-goal theory, relational theory, full range theory, transactional theory, and transformational theory (Jogulu & Wood, 2006). To have an understanding of transactional and transformational leadership theories, reviewing earlier leadership theories demonstrates the natural development that in time resulted in contemporary leadership theories.

Soonhee (2005) theorized that women leaders are not bound to traditional leadership styles and have become an asset to the survival and growth of the workplace and the success of the organization in which they serve. After studying leadership styles and theories, we will examine the factors governing women's leadership and decision styles, and their relationship to the voluntary employee turnover phenomenon.

Great Man Leadership Theory

Prior to the mid-20th century, the great man leadership theory was the foundation for the research of great leaders. Frequently, the great leaders were from the upper classes of society, although a few were from society's lower classes, which added to the perception that great leaders were born with leadership genes. According to

Jogulu and Wood (2006), the great man theory did not contribute to elevating the profile of women in management, because the theory was formulated as a male model at a time when women were not part of the workforce.

Trait Leadership Theory

As the prevalent leadership research in the 20th century, until the late 1940s and early 1950s, the trait theory is the psychological speculation that certain characteristics or traits are inherited. It speculated that if one were to study successful leaders, findings would reveal their individual leadership traits. If other people with the same traits could be found, then these people could also become great leaders. There are variations in this approach that depended on situations as well as the difficulty of the task. Jogulu and Wood (2006) decided that no conclusive evidence existed that the trait theory produces an increase in the number of women in management positions.

Path-Goal Leadership Theory

Helland and Winston (2005) posited that the path-goal theory emphasized the effects leaders' behaviors have on followers' satisfaction and the rewards available to them. Behavioral theory focused on determining what successful leaders have done, not what they are about to do (Torpman, 2004), and the assumption that leaders are made rather than born (Jogulu & Wood, 2006). The theory indicated that effective leaders can be molded by adopting specific styles and behaviors, and that leaders are not necessarily born with leadership qualities (Muller & Turner).

Contingency Era

In an attempt to improve organizational performance, Fiedler (1974) developed the Contingency Theory. Prior models that examined traits, behaviors, and situations could not adequately account for leadership effects on performance. Fiedler's contingency model emerged as the most researched leadership model during the 1970s (Bass, 1990). The basic insight of the model is that the relationship between leadership style and leadership effectiveness is contingent upon the specific demands of the situation (Vroom & Jago, 2007). Essentially, no one style of leadership is thought to be effective in all situations.

The contingency model led to the thinking that most people are effective in some leadership situations and ineffective in others. This view of leadership effectiveness led the way for Fiedler and others to suggest that leaders can improve their effectiveness by changing the situation rather than their personality or behavior (Vroom & Jago, 2007). Therefore, it is essential to study the situation to determine whether or not it fits the leader.

Relational Leadership Theory

The relational theory valued and encouraged diverse opinions and people in an attempt to accomplish change. In the relational theory, the leader is inclusive, purposeful, and ethical (Muller & Turner, 2005). The relational theory posited that a leader's ability to lead is dependent upon emotional intelligence. Webb (2009) and Muller and Turner characterized emotional intelligence as relationship competence and open-mindedness. Gordon and Grant (2005) suggested women leaders demonstrate the emotional intelligence to inspire and influence followers.

Full Range Leadership Theory

The full range theory of leadership (Avolio & Bass, 1995) was developed to broaden the range of leadership styles typically investigated in the field of leadership research. This theory challenges the conventions to present a concrete definition of leadership while highlighting qualities such as charisma and inspirational leadership as evaluation models and measures (Avolio & Bass, 1995).

The constructs comprising the full range leadership theory denote the three types of leadership behavior as transformational, transactional, and laissez-faire. These behaviors are described below:

Transactional Leadership Theory

Transactional leadership indicates an emphasis on maintaining the status quo of the organization and maintaining organizational practices and resources (Brownlee, Nailon, & Tickle, 2005). Transactional leadership theory builds on Bass's (1990) view that both leader and follower use each other to fulfill goals and objectives through the exchange of goods and services. Leader-follower relationships develop through a series of exchanges. Transactional leadership involves the leader rewarding or disciplining followers based on performance. Lemons and Parzinger (2008) suggested that the inherent qualities in women are more nurturing than men's and tend to support collaborative leadership concepts rather than transactional styles.

Laissez-Faire Leadership Theory

Lewin, Lippitt, and White (1939) conducted a study that resulted in one of the first references of the laissez-faire leadership style to examine the leadership within boys' clubs. The laissez-faire leadership style related to autocratic and democratic leadership styles. The study determined that autocratic leaders demonstrated more control over the laissez-fair leaders. Laissez-faire leaders adhere to the status quo and rarely interfere or cause conflict by introducing new strategy or organization direction.

In the laissez-fair approach, the leader has a more standoff approach to leading and allows subordinates to manage themselves. This approach works best in organizations that have a strong sense of self-direction and highly skilled workers who can manage their customers (Marques, 2006). The productivity, satisfaction, and cohesion of organizations led by laissez-faire leaders are hindered by leaders who are unable to provide sound direction (Bass, 1990).

Laissez-faire means "hands-off," which is truly the best way to describe this style of leadership. Leaders who operate using this method tend to distance themselves from their subordinates. They allow their staff to be independent and maintain their work without leadership interference. This leadership style only works well in specific environments with particular types of subordinates.

Transformational Leadership Theory

Transformational leadership is significant to leadership because of its application to current work situations (Avolio, Bhatia, Koh, & Zhu, 2004; Beng-Chong & Ployhart, 2004). Beng-Chong and Ployhart posited that since the changes within the economy affect organizations, leaders of organizations must contend to deal with the uncertainties in market fluctuation. A transformational leader must be able to view the organization as constantly reinvented to implement change when needed for improvement of the organization Sashkin, (1988).

An organization should be reviewed from a level that permits the vision and the future of the organization to be interpreted, with appropriate goals, objectives, and strategic plans being clearly set (Burns, 1978; McCabe & Naude, 2005; Russell & Tucker, 2004). Women display the traits of transformational leadership. A study by Groves (2005) discovered that women's extraordinary social and emotional competencies assist in appealing leadership behaviors.

Given the powerful effects of charismatic leadership on team cohesion, organizational performance, and follower performance and attitudes, women may indeed possess a decided advantage regarding the interpersonal skills and behaviors necessary for effective leadership in modern, change-oriented organizations (Groves, 2005, p. 40). Atwater, Avolio, and Bass (1996) found that men are more likely to display transactional leadership than women, while women tend to perform transformational leadership behaviors, particularly individualized consideration, more often than men. Atwater,

Avolio, and Bass (1996), Druskat (1994), and Rosener (1990) explored the gender aspects of leadership and found women are frequently seen by others and themselves as transformational leaders. These authors indicated women use transformational leadership styles more than men. In opposition, Komives (1991) and Maher (1997) found that transformational leadership is not influenced by gender. Carless (1998) and Gazso (2004) found that superiors rated female managers higher on transformational leadership while their subordinates rated men and women equally on transformational leadership style. Studies by Atwater et al., and Druskat, and Rosener may provide an understanding of how leadership styles have affected women leaders in Nigeria.

In contrast, men exceeded women on the transactional scales of management-by-exception and laissez-faire leadership. The results of these studies are inconsistent, but they do suggest that women score slightly higher on transformational leadership style assessments than men. The transformational leadership style encourages subordinates more than other leadership styles, which tend to be more authoritative. Furthermore, the results indicated that leaders using a transformational leadership style tend to be caring employers, whose employees are loyal and who remain faithful to the organization (Archambeau, 2006).

Women are occupying leadership roles traditionally occupied by men. As transformational leadership theory becomes more popular with organizations (Morrissey & Schmidt, 2008), the relationship between gender and leadership style has been an increasing topic of interest to organizations (Catalyst, 2005). The studies indicating a higher rating for women on the transformational scales are significant for the future of women executives (Morrissey & Schmidt, 2008). The increase of research results that point to a positive relationship between organizational success and transformational leadership is in contrast to results that indicate a negative relationship between management-by-exception passive leadership and laissez-faire leadership (Thyer, 2004).

The investigation on why women score higher than men on the measures of transformational leadership and effectiveness have launched several theories. One theory is that women have to meet higher standards than men to attain and retain leadership roles. Another theory states that women in management meet with resistance when they demonstrate the traditional authoritative styles. The possibility is that women leaders' gender role of socialization is similar with a transformational leadership style (Backhouse, Burns, Dani, & Masood, 2006).

Manning (2004) observed that transformational leaders typically nurture personal and group improvement, share inspiring organizational visions, and foster commitment and motivation toward important goals. A transformational leader helps people see the value in their contributions to the organization by increasing his or her levels of motivation (Hautala, 2005). Bass (1990) suggested transformational leaders inspire and motivate others to do more than followers originally intended to do or thought possible. Furthermore, Bass reiterated that leaders ought to strive to engage all members of the team in the decision-making process. He suggested transformational leaders create a workplace in which a follower considers placing group interests above individual interests for the good of the organization. Lemons and Parzinger (2008) maintained that females are better collaborators than males.

CHAPTER FIVE

CROSS-CULTURAL PERSPECTIVES ON MANAGEMENT AND LEADERSHIP

Twenty-first century studies of leadership has expanded to include perspectives focusing on the examination and comparison of cultural values and behaviors in different countries (Bass, Burger, Doktor, & Barrett, 1979, Bing, 2004 & Hofstede, 2001). Universal tendencies have been found among various countries, such as the United States and Britain to India and Japan, according to Bass et al. (1979), where organizational managers utilized a more proactive perspective in accomplishing tasks and less authority in their leadership approach. Bass (1990) examined countries in the Far East such as China, Southeast Asia, Japan, and Korea, and observed that these countries shared cultural values, a common religious belief, and traditional practices of Confucianism and Buddhism. To add to the cultural perspectives on leadership, Mom-Chhing (2009) posited that in comparison to American perspectives on leadership, Cambodian culture is authoritarian even though Cambodian organizational leaders based in the United States engaged in community decision-making.

One of the main debates among cross-cultural management scholars discussed how well the application of management practices may be transferred across cultures (Muenjohn & Armstrong, 2007). On one hand, scholars believed the significant changes in technology, communication, transportation, and free-market capitalism resulted in cultures becoming more alike because of the flat environment in which businesses are conducted today (Levitt, 1995). Organizational complexity further stems from interdependence among people, organizations, and nations, among various disciplines, and emerging technologies (Twomey, 2006). It was argued that culture was rooted in a deep value system that was unlikely to change; therefore, management practices needed to be tailor-made to fit diverse cultural backgrounds of leaders from diverse cultures (Hofstede, 1995). Other challenges encountered by organizational leaders include lack of authority and control, the need to answer to multiple stakeholders with diverse values, beliefs, ethnic and cultural backgrounds, and the lack of funding, staff, and resources (Silverman & Taliento, 2006).

Nigeria as a country with many cultures, religions, traditions and beliefs is not different in how the national culture affects the leadership and organizational practices of leaders. Zagoršek, Jaklič, & Stough (2003) conducted a study of three countries, Nigeria, Slovenia, and the United States, and observed the existence of great differences between cultures of the three countries. Nigeria scored highest on power distance and collectivism, because the country is moderately feminine and characterized by moderate uncertainty avoidance, similar to the United States. Slovenia classified as a highly collectivistic and feminine society characterized by a high uncertainty avoidance and power distance between leaders and workers (Zagoršek, Jaklič, & Stough). The United States was found to be the opposite: the culture was very individualistic, quite masculine, and a little below average on uncertainty avoidance and power distance. Slovenia and Nigeria appeared to be culturally closer to each other than to the United States (Zagoršek, Jaklič, & Stough).

In contrast, Terpstra (1978) in a study conducted on the universal tendencies found across countries, observed that there are unique cultural differences among different religions, customs, values, beliefs, attitudes, norms, language, education, wealth, social organization, politics, and law. These environmental factors were found to affect leader-follower relations, and these environmental factors dictated the way in which leaders exercised their leadership based on the culture of the environment in which they operate (Bass, 1990).

Countries in the Far East were found to place emphasis on the culture of collectivism and compliance with legitimate authority, while the culture of individualism and challenging authority was found to be prominent in Western countries, such as the United States (Bass, 1990).

In another study of leadership styles and cultural values of managers and subordinates in four countries, Kuchinke (2002) suggested that cross-cultural human resources development issues are not shaded in dual or multiple simplicities between the East and the West.

In-depth cross cultural leadership studies, such as those undertaken by Hofstede (2001) research, on the socio-cultural dimension focusing on the behavioral, social, and cultural variables in different countries, determined the socio-cultural value orientations of leaders. The value orientations of leaders, as posited by Hofstede (2001), are described as power distance, individualism, uncertainty avoidance, masculinity, and long-term orientation.

CHAPTER SIX

CULTURE AND LEADERSHIP STYLES

Rodriguez (1996) suggested that leaders who learn and interact with the culture of another country are more likely to develop a successful, long-term relationship because they have expanded their cultural understanding of another person or country's culture. Leaders who do not have a clear understanding of the national culture present in their environments can experience failures even with a good organizational strategy and plan in place (Beamish, Killing, Lecraw, & Morrison, 1994).

From a social perspective, culture is defined as a collective under-standing of a group that has different practices, beliefs, values, and norms from another (Hofstede, 1980). Aldag, Block, and Cunni-gham (1993) defined culture as the set of ideas, attitudes, behaviors, and values common to a group of people. Culture shapes the human behavior which is different from one society to another (Aldag et al., Aldag & Stern, 1991; Alvesson, 1993). The attitudes, behaviors, and values mentioned above take on added meaning with respect to time, language, and cultural context. This definition is consistent with other definitions that the culture of a nation defines behaviors, attitudes, and values of its members (Hunt, Osborn, & Shermerhorn, 1994; Newman & Nollen, 1996). Michael (1997) listed the cultural elements that affect management practices as (a) work values across cultures, (b) decision-making behaviors, (c) relationship-oriented behaviors, (d) communicating behaviors, and (e) influencing tactics. Grosse and Kujawa (1995) found that differences of cultures among employees affect communication, achievement, motivation, attitudes toward work, the concept of time, and hierarchical relationships.

Grosse and Kujawa hypothesized that aligning leaders and managers with subordinates on the dimensions of consideration and initiation structure would allow a leader to interact appropriately with the culture of the organization, sometimes based on environmental factors. In a 1999 study, Avkiran (1999) collected data from 102 Australian bank branches in which subordinates were asked to appraise the competence of their managers. Based on Avkiran's observation, a positive relationship was found between the concept of consideration in the form of interpersonal skills, which created an atmosphere of rapport and mutual trust, and the concept of participative management. According to Avkiran, this positive relationship would lead to job satisfaction and consequently greater effectiveness and performance within the organization.

Hofstede's Cross-Cultural Framework

Hofstede (1980, 1991, 1994, 2001) developed a cultural-dimension model based on a research study in 67 countries. He found five relationships that appear useful in describing the relationship of culture to management and leadership. In his studies, he observed the following five cultural dimensions can address changes of culture and management in society: power distance, individualism versus collectivism, masculinity versus femininity, and long-term versus short-term orientation. Hofstede's five dimensions are summarized as follows:

1. **Power Distance** describes the degree of inequality among people considered acceptable in society (Hofstede, 1994, 2001). The power distance is the extent to which a society accepts that power distributes unequally and measures the degree to which there is a psychological distance between a leader and its followers. Power distance is a continuum, with small power distance on the left and large power distance on the right (Hofstede, 1994, 55 2001).

   Leaders with small power distance would prefer the democratic approach to share power by everyone in the group. Leaders with high power distance tend to be autocratic with power centralized in the hands of a few, such as with the elite, based on class. This dimension refers to the comfort level that people have when in teracting and making decisions within the hierarchical structure of the organization.

High power distance is present when subordinates do not feel good about decisions made by leaders. Low power distance indicates that subordinates may wonder why leaders have a slow pace to decision making (Randolph & Sashkin, 2002). Power distance also refers to the perceptual inequality among people between different cultures (Hofstede, 1994). Societies that have high power distance tend to have a highly centralized management system (Zhang, 1994).

2. **Individualism and Collectivism** is the claim that the individual is the primary unit of reality and gives it the ultimate value, in contrast to collectivism, which maintains that the group holds the ultimate value and stresses the needs of the individuals as subordinate to those of the group.

From an individualist's point of view, an individual's primary goal is to deal with reality, while other people are simply one aspect of this reality. An individual's welfare is an end goal and should not sacrifice any individual for the sake of another. Collectivists look at reality as mediation among the group and consequently, give the group the authority to confront reality rather than the individual (Stata, 1992). Nigerian culture beliefs is of the collectivist view, since there is a huge national and family culture present in its leaders' practices.

Individualism started from the premise that to get to know the whole, it is necessary and sufficient to know the elementary or 56 atomic facts. It adopts the norm to tackle problems one at a time. Epistemological individualism focuses on the individual knower isolated from the learning community. It is true that cognition is a brain process, but individuals do learn from interaction with other group members (Bunge, 2000). Lee (1992) referred to individualism as a priority to personal goals over those of the group, while he referred to collectivism as the concept of giving priority to the group over the individual. The individualistic view of culture can be said to hold true for leaders of the 21st century and leaders in Nigeria, especially those belonging to the Generation X group. This dimension describes the level to which individualism and collectivism depend on the values of the society as well as other factors such as educational levels and subcultures within the organization (Lee, 1992).

3. **Masculinity versus Femininity** describes the degree to which society perceives values and traits as associated with masculine qualities. Masculine imagery is deprived of sensitivity towards themselves and others focused on the attainment of social status and material wealth; masculine males are expected to be independent and display assertiveness. In contrast, qualities of femininity include nurturance and sympathy (Hofstede, 1994, 2001). This dimension also describes the difference between the genders as well as the characteristics of one gender prevailing over the other (Hofstede, 1994). Masculinity refers to the degree to which certain values such as assertiveness, performance, and competitiveness prevail over feminine values such as quality of life, warm personal relationships, service, and solidarity (Hofstede, 1994).

Dimensions of masculinity are preferred in Nigerian society where males are favored in leadership positions. Certain professions are associated to masculine pride and preferably chosen for male members of the family rather than females. This aspect also holds true since the national culture in Nigeria functions in the masculine mode. Females are frowned upon when they occupy and manifest certain acts, roles, and leadership practices labeled as manly. When the assertiveness level is high, subordinates will not feel comfortable with a nurturing and relationship-oriented culture (Randolph & Sashkin, 2002). Nigerian culture believes in the collectivist view, since there is a huge national and family culture present in its leaders' practices.

(Rodriguez, 1996). European concepts of masculinity also fall in discord with the pre-colonial and post-colonial Nigerian cultural definition of manhood. European males are supposed to be assertive and tough while the European females are modest and tender.

Nigerian gender roles factor sex for the purpose of procreation. Gender attributes are relevant, but above all Nigerian culture in the pre-colonial era measured women's ability and capability in contributing to maintaining the existence of the family, groups, and nation. In post-colonial Nigerian culture, there is a clear contrast between mores that are adopted from European influence and traditional customs that honor a woman's leadership capacity.

4. **Uncertainty Avoidance** describes the extent to which a person can deal with threatening, ambiguous, or anxiety-provoking situations. Strong uncertainty avoidance is associated with traditional cultures, while weak uncertainty avoidance is associated with contemporary cultures (Hofstede, 1994, 2001). This dimension describes the amount of uncertainty that can coexist with the amount of tolerance people can have for uncertain situations (Hofstede, 1994, 2001). A high-level of uncertainty avoidance indicates that subordinates prefer carefully detailed goals, assignments, policies, and procedures. In low levels of uncertainty avoidance, subordinates can tolerate unclear descriptions of the goals, processes, and procedures.

The leadership of an organizaion should be mindful not to empower subordinates too quickly without proper training to measure capacity. A low-level of uncertainty avoidance can lead to chaos if presented in an environment in which subordinates prefer clarity (Randolph & Sashkin, 2002). Organizations with high uncertainty avoidance culture adhere to the organizational hierarchy in management, processes, rules, and regulations (Zhang, 1994). Therefore, leaders can introduce mechanisms to reduce risks because subordinates are threatened by uncertainty (Michael, 1997).

5. **Long-term and Short-term Orientation** refers to the degree to which organizations adopt either long-term or short-term performance strategies (Hofstede, 2001, Hunt et al., 1991). This cultural dimension is derived from the research done by Michael Bond. He used the Chinese values survey in support of Confucian dynamism and focused on relationships, thrift, a sense of shame, personal steadiness, reciprocity, and respect for tradition (Hunt et al., 1991). Long-term orientation reflects persistence, perseverance, and thrift as compared to short-term orientation that reflects personal stability, respect, tradition, and fulfilling social expectations (Hofstede).

Hofstede stated that Long-Term Orientation stands for the fostering of virtues, rewards, perseverance, and thrift. Its opposite pole, Short-Term Orientation, stands for the fostering of virtues related to the past and present; in particular, respect for tradition, preservation, and fulfilling social obligations. Hoppe (1990) conducted a study that was the first comprehensive follow-up on Hofstede's (1980) germinal work on international differences in work-related values. The main purpose of the study was to test the construct validity of Hofstede's Four-D model. The secondary goal was to explore statistical relationships between Hofstede's value dimensions of uncertainty avoidance and masculinity and A. Kolb and D. Kolb's (2001) experiential learning model. The results largely supported the validity of Hofstede's dimensions even though the dimension of masculinity showed weaker relationships with the study's results.

Ardichvili and Kuchinke (2002) provided important insight into the validity of the models, even though it may not cover the universe in regards to socio-cultural dimensions relevant to leadership. Grouping countries based on cultural, geographic, or religious proximity could be equally questionable. For example, one may expect that

Thailand, Cambodia, and Laos would form a homogeneous subset because of proximity and sharing of similar religious beliefs (Mom-Chhing, 2009). These countries are quite different. Regional differences within a country may also influence leadership style.

Another example is that one may expect Nigeria to have the same culture throughout the country, but the national culture is different from family culture or other traditional practices that vary from each Nigerian society or community to the other. Therefore, leadership and management development recommendations based on country profiles and grounded in Hofstede's dimensions should be taken with caution to ensure their validity. According to Bing (2004), Hofstede's work provided practical applications in cross cultural training and development to help people work more effectively in more than one culture. Application of dimensions can help people understand their cultural tendencies. Regarding models of leadership, organizational leaders need to understand that leadership practices and expectations may differ internationally, regionally, and even locally.

CHAPTER SEVEN

CULTURE AND LEADERSHIP IN THE 21ST CENTURY

Globalization is bringing leaders across the globe together to achieve common goals within their organizations—to remain effective and be able to compete in an innovative 21st century. However, a person's national culture may be different from the leadership practice of the 21st century. Therefore, authors arguing that there are universal perspectives in leadership need to understand local and cultural practices that dictate many leadership styles (Okpara, 2007). The national and family culture present may be preventing the next generation of future leaders, specifically those belonging to the Generation X group, to fully adapt to innovative 21st century leadership (Okpara).

Two studies reflected opposing views on the nature of a person's cultural influence on his or her leadership style (Hanges, Lord et al.). The underlying argument in these studies stated that in an organization, the environmental factors present in the society affect the leadership practices of leaders. Hanges, Lord et al. posited that an appropriate leadership style or practice in one culture may not be appropriate in another.

National Culture

Zagoršek (2005) observed that the effectiveness of leadership is unique and depends on the national culture. A person's beliefs, values, ideals, religion, and norms are deeply rooted in his leadership practices, and national culture affects the leadership behavior, styles, goals, structure, culture, and strategies of organizations. Newman (1996) stated that understanding the national culture is central to organizing a core belief of a person's leadership style.

An acceptable way or practice of leadership in one culture may not be preferred in another. Social psychologists argue that culture is socialized in a person through the shared values of social groups that in turn play key roles in a person's cognitive, emotional, and social functioning (Cooper & Denner, 1998; Markus & Kitayama, 1991; & Triandis, 1989). These socialization patterns, in turn, shape how people perceive self and others.

Family Culture

Ejiofor (1987) stated that cultural factors affect leadership in many ways. He argued that leaders, especially within the extended family system, see themselves as working for members of the family as well as the extended family, rather than for his or her immediate gratification. In a culturally inclusive society, organizational leaders view themselves based on their family name, responsibilities, and the societal construct of how a man or woman should or should not behave among peers, subordinates, and others in the work environment. Decision-making relies on patrilineal family and social structures, and many people have to base their leadership styles on the national and family culture of the country (Okpara, 2007). Therefore, national culture affects the personality, attitudes, and behaviors of a leader or person in positions of power.

Previous studies relating cultural issues to work behaviors, such as with those in leadership, have concluded that cultural factors influence a person's leadership style (Ahiauzu, 1984; Ejiofor, 1987; & Okpara, 1996). Pekerti (n.d) stated that universalities and culture-specificities are more likely to be found than not, in places where family culture and tradition are very strong (Holmberg & Åkerblom, 2007; Keller, 2003; Kriger & Seng, 2005). Previous studies confirmed the notion that perceptions of what makes an effective and ineffective leader are similar in content across cultures, with variations of what is important, especially between cultures sharing an overarching value structure, such as religion (Abdalla & Al-Homoud, 2001; Bryman, 1987; Dastmalchian et al., 2001; Kriger & Seng, 2005; Pasa et al., 2001). At the same time, there are large variations on how people perceive leadership in cultures different from one another (Dastmalchian et al., 2001; Ling et al., 2000).

The national and family culture is one that values collectivism more than individualism. The national culture of work and leadership practices is based on the beliefs and practices of collectivism. This collectivist culture is deeply rooted in the colonial construct carried over into the 21st century, where women were grouped into subordinate roles.

Influences of Gender and Culture on Leadership

In a review of 162 studies examining leadership styles across genders, Eagly & Johnson (1990) indicated that the proportion of gender comparisons stereotypical in direction differed significantly from the results expected. According to Eagly & Johnson (1990), the strongest evidence obtained in gender difference in leadership style occurred in women's tendency to adopt a more democratic or participatory style of leadership and for men to adopt a more autocratic or directive style.

Ninety-two percent of the available comparisons found more democratic behavior came from women than from men. Similarly, Rosner (1990) conducted an investigation of female leaders from four continents and discovered they all encouraged participation, shared power, energized, and enhanced the self-worth of others. Therefore, women are expected to engage in leadership practices that enable others to act and encourage the hearth more often than men will.

Transformational Leadership in a Cross-Cultural Setting

A study conducted by Spreitzer, Perttula, & Xin (2005) in the United States and Taiwan found that cultural values in these countries play a significant role in the relationships between transformational leadership and organizational effectiveness. Madzar (2005) maintained that transformation leadership is a meaningful determinant of subordinates seeking information from organization leaders. According to Bass (1997), transformational leadership should be consistent across world cultures.

Studies examining the relationships between culture and transformational leadership are limited (Muenjohn & Armstrong, 2007). Many of these studies were conceptual investigations on different cultural characteristics. These studies were based on their reviews. Jung, Bass, and Sosik (1995) conceived that characteristics of collectivistic cultures can enhance an easier emergence of transformational leadership than those of individualistic cultures. The basic behaviors present in transformational leadership, such as motivation, inspiration, intellectual challenge, and individual consideration, were seen as necessary components of leadership around the world (Dorfman, 1996).

This notion stated that transformational leaders were more effective than those who displayed transactional or non-leadership behaviors, regardless of culture, organization, or country. Bass (1997) also observed that there is a universal culture that applies to many organizations regardless of their national culture.

CHAPER EIGHT

GENERATION X

Generation X is broadly defined as unfocused and apathetic and includes people born between 1961 and 1981. Literature published in the late 1990s primarily highlighted a negative portrait of Generation X and described its members as young adults seeking balance, flexibility, and financial stability (Zill & Robinson, 1997). Members of Generation X grew up in the 1970s and 1980s, in the wake of the revolution of the 1960s. Societal traditions had altered; a person's rank at birth was no longer the predictor of one's ultimate place in the socio-economic structure (Dunne, 1997). Generation Xers are characterized as shallow, politically apathetic, illiterate, and disloyal (Bernardi & Mahedi, 1994; Strauss & Howe, 1991). Generation X is comprised of practical leaders who are determined to take control of their destinies and raise the entrepreneurial bar by developing new approaches to leadership (Dunne, 1997).

Economically, those belonging to the Generation X group entered the workforce during the period of productivity decline in which many women had carriers, were independent, and could fend for themselves economically. This is in contrast to the previous Baby Boomer generation, where tangible wages were stagnant and opportunities for career advancement were not consistent (Levy, 1999). Additionally, confidence in the long-term sustainable employment opportunities has diminished in the minds of Generation Xers because they witnessed their parents get laid off mid-career due to corporate downsizing (Howe & Strauss, 1993). When it comes to planning, baby boomers aim for the long term, but Generation Xers are different. While Baby Boomers planned over a scope of 50 years, Generation Xers have reduced their plans to a 3 or 5-year span. Some describe Generation Xers as angry because of their lack of long-term projection and stability (Dunne, 1987).

Generation Xers defy traditional market strands and have moved to forge their ways to create new economic opportunities. Generation Xers have also made improvements in the measuring scopes used to grade economic market progress world-wide. They have used the world of information technology to shorten the widening gap caused by distance and time travel and to stay above the competing older generation (Dunne, 1987).

Rather than facing the obstacles of the organizational hierarchy, members of Generation X are most likely to create new organizations to rid the constraints and conventions established by previous generations. Generation Xers attack a posing problem as a whole rather than in parts to include solutions for social set-backs, to protect the environment, and to salvage communal values through redevelopment projects that revitalize abandoned industries (Dembner, 1998).

General Characteristics of Generation X

Generation X is made of many different subgroups who have managed to work in cohesion and project a semblance of homogeneity; they are individuals with the drive to move forth and the ambition to embark on a quest (Paulin & Riordon, 1998, p. 11). Rice (1995) defined the following four distinguishing categories to describe different backgrounds and beliefs of Generation X: "(a) cynical disdainers, (b) traditional materialists, (c) hippies revisited, and (d) fifties machos." First, the group of cynical disdainers is characterized as "pessimistic and skeptical…. receiving most of the press attention" (p. 114). Second, traditional materialists compare to the "Baby Boomer generation, [displaying a] positive and optimistic attitude, striving for the American Dream" (p. 114). Third, "the group of hippies revisited replays the lifestyles and values of the sixties and expresses itself through music, fashion, and spirituality" (p. 115). Fourth, "the fifties machos are conservatives, who believe in stereotyped gender roles and are the least accepting of multiculturalism" (p. 114).

Different generations frequently contribute specific characteristics in the available literature, including historical handbooks, novels, and journals, intending to secure the fundamental nature and values of a period (Brinkley, 1994). Brinkley stated that the idiom "Generation X [carried] all the germs of propaganda and stereotype" (p. 1). The recession and Generation Xers' embarrassment about their compromised 1960s values caused this behavior. Georges (1994) contended that "It's the first generation to live so well and complain about it" (p. 27).

According to Celek and Zander (1996), empirical records provide information about young adults being equally confident about a positive development for the future economic situation as other generations. Ladd (1994) concluded that "Claims of sharp generational differences and conflict may make good copy, but they are rarely justified" (p. 18). Howe and Strauss (1992) commented in *The New Generation Gap*: "this generation—more accurately this generation's reputation--has become a Boomer metaphor for America's loss of purpose, disappointment with institutions, despair over the culture and fear for the future" (p. 88). This theme proposed to view the culture of Generation X only as an indicator for an even more profound disorder in the postmodern world, and that isolation could also affect generations not characterized as Generation X.

Tulgan maintained members of Generation X are not inherently doubtful, but manifest disbelief as a reaction to the moral decline in all aspects. Coupland deduced that general pessimism was the consequent reaction of excessive and misleading advertising of consumer goods in the 1980s.

Generation X Leaders

According to Ansoorian, Good, and Samuelson (2003), it is necessary to clarify the significant differences that exist between Generation X and baby boomers to delineate tension that may arise in future social and working relationships between the two groups. In *Fortune Magazine* (Watson, 2002) proclaimed that Generation X, having grown up during the most profound changes in the economy after the industrial revolution, is a "wrecked generation" (p. 60). Although Generation X is the most highly educated generation ever, with approximately 60% having some college education, it is also the first generation likely to have a standard of living below that of its parents (Codrington, 1998). Leon (cited in Tapscott, 2001) stated that, for the next 50 years, Generation X will be running the world's businesses, but they will be questioned if they have what it takes to be successful. "Leadership in business is much more about communication and credibility than it is about procedure and policy...What you are is every bit as important, and sometimes more, than what you know" (p. 5).

Foley and LeFevre (2000) concluded Generation X members are survivors who have had to deal with familial and social relationships that differ from that of previous generations. For example, many had to face coming home to an empty home or having to fend for oneself and siblings at a very young age. Generations Xers have also had to deal with the highest divorce rate in history, yet remain optimistic in romanticizing personal desires for lasting personal and romantic relations. Such independence feeds the assumption that no one owes Generation X members a job, a belief that led to a highly competitive work ethic in this generation. One could argue that Generation X is equipped to tackle the competitive nature of the business, as well as to bring creativity, initiative, and a close-the-deal mentality to the industry (Levy, 1999).

Generation X employees have joined the workforce of the 21st century postmodern economy. However, unlike the Baby Boomer generation, Generation Xers do not seek lifelong employment; instead, they seek lifelong learning opportunities. According to Elsdon and Iyer (1999), Generation X values employability, not sheer employment itself. They have taken charge of their paths and destinies and placed value on autonomy and independence.

Zemke et al. (2000) found that there has been a shift from the status of employment to the status of being employable. An employable workforce with excellent interpersonal skills and superb theoretical and practical knowledge based on education and professional experience is especially precious to organizations. "Never have so few been wanted by so many" (p. 42).

Tulgan (2000) expanded on the mind-set of Generation X by drawing attention to their performance: "Tell me what to do, give me the information, and then let me create" (p. 46). Generation X employees carefully plan their careers. They are aware that there will be no lifetime employment, but that they have the responsibility to remain employable. The "technologically savvy, fickle, ultra-mobile Generation X workforce value self-advancement over corporate advancement. They view their human capital as personal, not corporate asset" (Harari, 1998, p. 25). Kronenberg (1997) supported this statement with the observation that it is common for Generation X employees to change employers every 18 months.

As employees, Generation X possesses the necessary skills coupled with wide range knowledge stemming from various sources; they are valuable in the workforce. Beware of Generation X, because they offer zero stability and often leave employers without assets they created (Vollmer & Phillips, 2000).

Employers are now faced with the challenge to provide Generation Xers with a workplace setting that is financially lucrative, and that fulfills ambitions and growth. Generation Xers look for work that will satisfy their curiosity, ambition, financial needs, and desire for growth while allowing them to balance family life and the workplace. They are not part of the obedient and unquestionable crowd; as employees, Generation Xers want to speak freely. Take away all these provisions and they will walk out and move on to the next workplace (Hessen & Lewis, 2001).

Challenges to Generation X Women in Leadership

Women and leadership are an important social concern (Nwosu, 2006). Women in the 21st century have contributed notably to various organizations and have ascended to top leadership positions in their respective businesses and professions. Despite this escalation in rank, many women in positions of power face enormous problems in their abilities to lead organizations effectively based on societal values, norms, and beliefs.

During colonial times, women's roles became limited to domestic labor. Europeans introduced cultural mores as a way of life to degrade and decapitate women's status. In the post-colonial era, women became decision-makers. Several social factors—such as the level of education, family background, exposure to young women in their families attaining leadership positions, their social backgrounds, the professional sector or business in which they work, and whether or not there are young women in leadership positions in their businesses—reflect how men, previous generations of women in leadership positions, and those in the immediate family background treat Generation X women in leadership positions.

Environmental awareness to women's issues, such as women's rights and equality campaigns in the national culture, also determine how others view or treat Generation X women in leadership positions. Post-colonial women own and empower themselves through various activities and leadership styles. Their governance directly relates to the change in cultural, societal messages. Women belonging to the Generation X sub-culture rightfully and naturally benefit from tradition restored, and their leadership roles have emerged to surpass superficial barriers and to sustain pre-colonial privileges.

However, a problem exists for women leaders. Women in key leadership positions often face many burdens because they have responsibilities to their families, professions, and other activities (Division for the Advancement of Women, 2005; Okeskalago, 2008;

Okome, 2002; Osiruemu, 2004). Obstacles rooted in colonial ruling practices counter their progress. These obstacles are carried over to infiltrate and dominate modern day organizational and social structures based on societal misfits. Other problems affecting the leadership styles of women in positions of power include religious practices or mores, limited resources, broken down social support, and networking structures. Furthermore, women in positions of power are not given full access to networks, and they often do not receive the leadership support and mentorship needed for growth.

Many modern women leaders have to adapt to changing organizations, as well as balance their leadership styles based on the general societal expectations from a male-dominated society. All these problems hinder the leadership styles of women in positions of power and paralyze their abilities to lead organizations effectively in a 21st century global context.

Women Leaders and Generational Influence

Women between the ages of 40 to 45 who use the transformational leadership style are closely related in age to Baby Boomers, and have learned from that generation. For the baby boomer generation, filial duties based on family and societal mores prevent them from being as independent as Generation X women, who can delay being in the family duty. Thus, it can be assumed that environmental adaptation to global and environmental trends assists Generation X women in positions of power to exercise various leadership styles that are not based on national or family culture, but on the organizational environment. This is coupled with the ease of Generation X women in positions of power to adapt to the current global business culture of working with diverse groups of people. Unlike previous generations of women in similar positions, Generation X women leaders learn about and adapt new technologies in their everyday lives and make better independent choices.

Organizational leaders, conducting business internationally or in cross-cultural environments, understand the lived-experiences of Generation X women in positions of leadership so that they do not fail in efforts to improve organizational goals and strategies. The goals and strategies of organizations improve in instances where the workforces are diversified to include younger generations of leaders, such as women and those from various multi-cultural backgrounds. Organizational goals and strategies also improve when business leaders understand how Generation X women working in a multi-cultural environment view and use power in day-to-day leadership positions (Chan & Mauborgne, 2009).

Challenges such as financial empowerment, views by men and older generations, competition for promotion within the organization, ascribed and prescribed roles of women leaders, societal norms, and family values are some of the obstacles Generation X women in positions of power face. However, many women in the Generation X group are breaking away from these filial and society norms, which often relegate women to the backgrounds and limit their power in the society.

While the research for the case study of this book was conducted amongst Nigerian women in leadership positions, challenges or inequality of women and leadership is a cross-cutting issue across the globe and is applicable as a similar cross-cultural leadership theme where women and those interested in the advancement of women will benefit from the added research. According to Bing (2004), Hofstede's work provided practical applications in cross-cultural training and development to help people work more effectively in more than one culture. Application of dimensions can help people understand their own cultural tendencies.

CHAPTER NINE

WOMEN'S LEADERSHIP IN A GENERATION X CULTURE

The role of culture on the leadership styles of Generation X women is seen as an emerging trend in which younger generations of women are ascending the professional ladder faster. More women are earning higher incomes, leading organizations, and traveling more than in previous generations. This progress for some of the world's women is hindered by various obstacles, though. Challenges such as financial empowerment, views by men and older generations, competition for promotion in the organization, ascribed and prescribed roles of women, societal norms, and family values are some of the issues Generation X women in positions of power face. Many women in the Generation X group have broken away from norms, and most do not consider their cultural values while leading their organizations.

Many women in the Generation X group respect culture and understand their roles within the family and in the society. How many of the Generation Xers in leadership positions lead organizations in the 21st century is influenced by their knowledge of worldviews, pop culture, and the fast-paced business environment. The participants for this study believed that with better knowledge of globalization issues and how they affected younger generations, Generation X women in positions of power could use the opportunity of achieving a higher education as a tool to fight oppression and achieve equality. This further knowledge and education can be viewed as a correlation to their selected leadership style. The more knowledge and education she possesses, the better a Generation X woman can be assertive in her opinions to speak her mind.

Generation X women in positions of power are judged and pressured to accept western leadership practices depending on the sector in which they work. Most were happy to accept emerging trends and views of organizational leadership to make their work run smoother and to lead organizations effectively. Many, on the other hand, believed that the job sector, the type of team or staff they led, and the organizational culture depicted their leadership styles.

In *Generation X: The Role of Culture on the Leadership Styles of Women in Leadership Positions*, we explored the day-to-day leadership styles of Generation X women in positions of power and how culture affects the leadership styles of these women. It was found that there were differences in opinions from men, previous generations, and peers about Generation X women in leadership positions. We also discovered that learning about different leadership styles of Generation X women was an emerging trend. Generation X women have differing views about their positions of power depending on the professional sector and culture of the area that they work in.

Others' treatment of Generation X women's leadership differs based on several demographics of men, previous generations of women leaders, and subordinates. These demographic factors include (a) levels of education, (b) family background, (c) exposure to young women attaining leadership positions, (d) social backgrounds, (e) the professional sector or business in which these women work, and (f) the presence or absence of young women in leadership positions in their places of work (g). Environmental awareness of women's issues also determines how others view and treat Generation X women in leadership positions.

Equality for women on the job is a wide-spread issue across different countries, where women are fighting to attain higher levels of leadership. However, several factors, including increasing understanding of women's issues, are changing previous views of Generation X women leaders.

The younger the generation of men and subordinates that work for Generation X women, the better the Generation X women in power are treated. Older generations of women still have a traditionalist view of the societal culture and assigned roles of women in the society.

The significance of the emerging leadership of Generation X women in society shows that more people, especially younger generations, are welcoming more women leaders. Society has a diversified world view and a better perspective on how women, in general, and particularly those in the Generation X sub-group, can be effective in managing organizations amidst prevalent national and societal cultures.

Generation X women's leadership styles vary depending on the culture of the organization they lead and the types of people that they manage on a day-to-day basis. From the results of this study, many of the participants between 34-39 years of age were comfortable with the democratic style of leadership, because they liked working with people in diverse environments by giving everyone the opportunity to add to organizational goals. Those who selected the situational style of leadership explained that the opportunity to exercise different leadership styles was based on their professional sector, region, and customer base and the day-to-day activities within the organizational environment, and not based on societal and cultural values or norms. Data from the study also signified that the older the Generation X women in positions of power are, the more they use the transformational leadership style based on their professional and family experiences in the society.

Participants between the ages of 40 to 45 who selected the transformational leadership style were closely related in age to the baby boomers and had learned from that generation. Also, the study observed that even when Generation X women are bound by the family or national culture of their country, they are more outgoing than baby boomers and can easily adapt to the organizational culture. Thus, it can be assumed from the findings of the study that environmental adaptation to global and environmental trends assists Generation X women in exercising various leadership styles that are not based on national or family culture, but on that of the organizational environment. However, with the ease of adapting to trends in the current global business climate, Generation X women are able to work with diverse groups of people. Learning about and adapting new technologies to their everyday lives and possessing an ability to make better independent choices also sets Generation X apart from previous generations of women in similar positions.

CASE STUDY:
Women and Leadership in Nigerian Organizations

The purpose of this phenomenological qualitative study was to investigate the leadership styles of Nigerian women belonging to the Generation X sub-culture. An open-ended survey questionnaire consisting of 10 demographic questions and 15 open-ended questions was used in interviewing participants for the study. Question 11 in the open-ended question was left as an attribute in that section. Therefore, there were 14 open-ended questions with one question as an attribute. The intent was to understand participants' perspectives and interpret perceptions of the role of culture on the leadership characteristics of Generation X women in Nigeria.

The sample drawn for the study was women between the ages of 30 and 45. Overall, 50 participants were interviewed for the study, which included the pilot study and post data questionnaire follow up. Thirty participants were interviewed for the research, while 20 people participated in providing feedback for the two pilot studies conducted. While this sample does not reflect the leadership styles or opinion of every single Nigerian woman in leadership positions or provide background information on the leadership and decision-making choices of women around the world, the number needed for a phenomenological study was fulfilled with the 30 participants involved in the research.

Based on the problem statement, the research questions for this case study were as follows:

1. What are the general attitudes of peers and subordinates toward Generation X women in positions of power?

2. What role does societal (national and family) culture play on the leadership styles of Generation X women?

3. How do Generation X women in positions of power view and use power within the organization?

Pilot Study

Cooper and Schindler (2002) stated, "A pilot test is conducted to detect weakness in design and instrumentation… One form of pre-testing may rely on colleagues, respondent surrogates, or actual respondents to refine a measuring instrument" (p. 86). Prior to conducting the actual interview, 10 participants were selected at random to provide feedback on the questionnaire format while another 10 provided feeback both on format and content.

The pilot study was conducted over a one-week period. Based on feedback from the pilot study, the researcher was able to modify the questionnaire format and questions. Conducting a pilot study prior to the data collection period assisted the researcher in re-writing the questionnaire to include more choice answers for survey partici-pants. Feedback from the pilot study assisted in revising the open-ended questionnaire format. The questionnaire was divided into two parts and the researcher made changes to include question 11 as an attribute in the open-ended question section. The first ten questions were based on Generation X women and power while the last five questions were based on the different leadership styles of Genera-tion X women located in Nigeria. An open-ended questionnaire was appropriate for a qualitative study; an assumption into phenomeno-logical study was that the research questions became the primary in-strument for data gathering for the research study (Creswell, 2002).

Data Collection

Data collection was conducted among Nigerian women who were in business, management, and leadership positions in various sec-tors across Nigeria. The data collection process was carried out to give participants a better understanding about the research topic and the purpose of the research. Those eligible for the proposed research were selected based on already established criteria that included individuals belonging to the Generation X group or being between the ages of 30 to 45. Pseudonyms such as 001 to 030 were assigned to the questionnaires to protect the identity of the participants. Data collection began with an overview of demographic survey of 10 general questions relating to participant's age group, region, ethnic group, level of education, position in the organization, and years of experience in leadership post, number of people responsible for supervising, annual salary range, religious background, and family background.

Data Analysis

Data analysis entails "discovering themes from the data…answering the major research questions and forming an in-depth understanding of the central phenomenon" (Creswell, 2002, p. 265). By using the themes and invariant constituents as recommended by Moustakas (1994), individual textural descriptions were constructed. These descriptions included full description of participants' perceptions, experiences, ideas, and beliefs (including feelings), and opinions. The purpose of the reviews and analysis was to develop individual textural descriptions as was suggested by Moustakas (1994).

As suggested by Siegle (2006), a method of member validation was necessary to ensure validity. Data for the study was presented using Moustakas' (1994) modified Van Kaam method of phenomenological presentation and Creswell (2005) steps as follows: (a) listing and grouping, (b) reduction and eliminating, (c) clustering, (d) identifying themes by application, (e) theme validation, (f) textual description, and (g) textual and structural description. The demographic section of the survey was analyzed using the Statistical Package for the Social Sciences (SPSS) while the open–ended part was transcribed using the NVIVO 9 software.

Study Demographics

The study sample for this section of the study consisted of 30 participants ranging in age from 30 to 45 years. Thirteen of the participants were between the ages of 30 to 34. Ten of them were between the ages of 35 to 39. Two of them were between the ages of 40 to 44, while five of the research participants were between the ages of 45 and over. Based on the six geo-political zones of Nigeria, participants hailed from four of them. Seven participants were from the North–Central zone, four were from the South–South, nine were from the South–East while 10 were from the South-West. The research study was opened to all ethnic groups and regions of Nigeria, the researcher did not have any participants from the North-North, and North–East regions.

Although all participants were of the Christian faith, and most were from the South, East, West, and Middle–Belt regions, some of the research participants worked in the Northern part of the country. The participants who worked in the Northern–Muslim part of Nigerian selected the situational style of leadership based on the educational level, religious beliefs, moral values and cultural norms of the Northern–Muslim part of the country. As far as the highest level of education completed, 12 of the participants obtained a Bachelor's degree, 13 obtained a Master's degree, and one obtained a doctorate, while the other four participants obtained other degrees. Out of the 30 participants, 12 were in management positions, two were in executive positions, five were business owners, one was a partner in her organization, and nine of the participants were associated while one held a position as senior associate with her organization.

Bar Chart

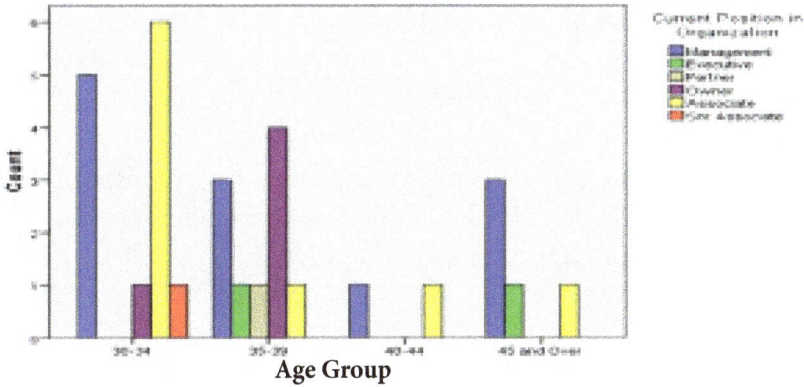

Age Group

Fig. 1

The minimum requirement to participate in the research was to have one year of leadership experience in a business or organization and people management skills. The research participants were all experienced professionals whether in their private businesses or working in an organization. Out of the 30 participants, 19 of them had at least five years of leadership experience, seven of them had at least 10 years of leadership experience, two had at least 15 years of leadership experience and one had over 20 years of leadership experience. When it came to the number of people the respondents managed on the job, 14 of them managed, at least five people, eight of them managed 10 people, one of them managed 15 people, two people of the participants managed 20 people, while five of the respondents managed over 20 people. The data from the pilot study of 20 participants were not reflected in the final data analysis of this research since the pilot study tested the feasibility of the current study under investigation.

All participants were from middle or upper-class families, with 28 of them from middle–class families and two from upper-class families. The annual salary range of the participants was between $25,000 and over $55,000. Eleven of the participants earned salaries of under $25,000, and five of them earned between $25,000 and $40,000. Three of the respondents earned between $40,000 and

$55,000 while 11 of the participants earned over $55,000. The survey interview was open to all faith, religious, economic, social and ethnic backgrounds but all the participants, irrespective of the zones or regions that they were from, were Christians. There were no participants of Muslim, African Traditional Religion (ATR), or other faiths in the study. There were, however, several participants who worked with peers and subordinates with different religious, economics or faith backgrounds in the study.

Findings and Themes

This part of the data analysis demonstrated how participants responded to the primary research questions. When answering these questions, participants disclosed their lived experiences and perceptions and how they related to each of the primary research questions for the study. The information gathered allowed for an accurate representation of the data. From the study outcome, three general themes emerged based on the research questions. These three themes are: (a) There are clear differences in opinions and perspectives of Generation X women in leadership positions compared to those of previous generations and men, (b) leadership of Generation X women in Nigeria is still an emerging trend, and (c) the leadership styles or characteristics of Generation X women are different from previous generations.

Several sub-themes, as shown in the diagrams, emerged from each of the research questions and general themes.

Primary Research Question One: *What are the general attitudes of peers and subordinates, including men, toward Generation X women in positions of power?*

The intent of this question was to understand the treatment by peers and subordinates in the organizational environment, and how those in the immediate organizational environment view and treat young women leaders in Nigeria who exhibit different or certain leadership styles. The following sub-themes emerged as shown in Figure 2.

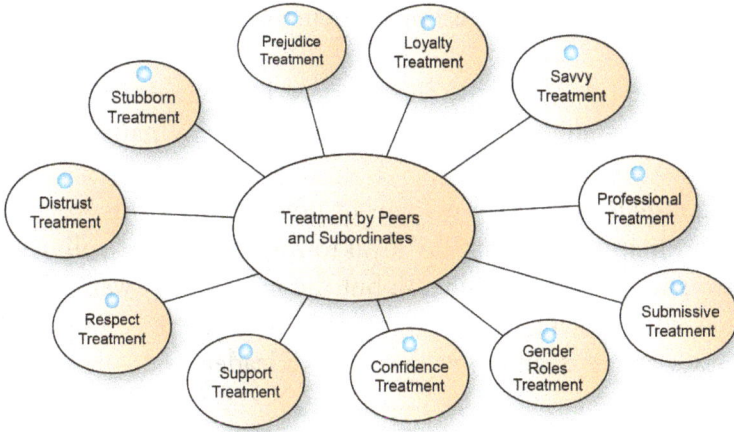

Fig. 2

Theme One: *There are clear differences in perspectives and opinions of previous generations of women leaders and men in Nigeria on the leadership styles of Generation X women.*

The general theme of this question was that there are clear differences and perspectives on the opinions of Generation X women in positions of power compared to those in the baby boomer generation, or men. Some of the responses to *Question One* are listed below:

> *Respondent 001:* "To me when you are professional, gender will play a lesser role; in other words, both men and women alike will look beyond gender once you do your job right."

> *Respondent 002:* "Women are skeptical, confrontational and judgmental. The men are divided: some are very loyal, supportive, cooperative and very helpful. The other men are difficult, rude and impossible."

Respondent 003: "They treat me with respect, but the women seem to think that I should be more sympathetic when they are late to work and give reasons for being late."

Respondent 004: "Mostly with respect; however, some see me as competition and being in a hurry to take over a man's world."

Respondent 005: "As a woman of power within the group, the subordinates always appear loyal to my office, where all usually seems well on the peripheral; but the men always want to exert their domineering attitudes, whereas the women run their conspiracy sessions, all in my absence as a leader."

Respondent 006: "They see Generation X women as a threat and believe that they have come to take their jobs."

Respondent 008: "They find it difficult to accept you as a leader. They believe you are too young for the leadership position."

Respondent 009: "As a woman in leadership, I have personally received more support from men. The view is that because I'm a woman, I am probably not as strong, and should be propped and aided. There's been more difficulty with the women, and I guess that boils down to uncouth competitiveness. 'If she can do it, why can't I?' As much as competition is good, I reckon the emotional nature of women does not enable them to be detached from the fight, hence the aggression and perceived rudeness and difficulty."

Respondent 017: "With respect and encouragement—they expect that I will do better than they did because I now have more opportunities than they did."

Respondent 023: "They treat me well so long as I don't look down on them and I seek their opinions. When I need to differ from their opinions, I sometimes take the time to explain why I need to take this other course and not what they advised. I work well with them."

Primary Research Question Two: *What role does societal culture play on the leadership styles of Generation X women in Nigeria?*

This question was asked to understand the day-to-day lived experiences from participant's views. These day-to-day lived experiences includes challenges, obstacles, positive and negative outcomes of how their leadership style was influenced or not by their cultural beliefs, societal norms, religious practices, and family values. This question was asked to understand the role of how societal values expect Generation X women in positions of power to behave regardless of their positions of power. The following sub-themes emerged as shown in Figure 3.

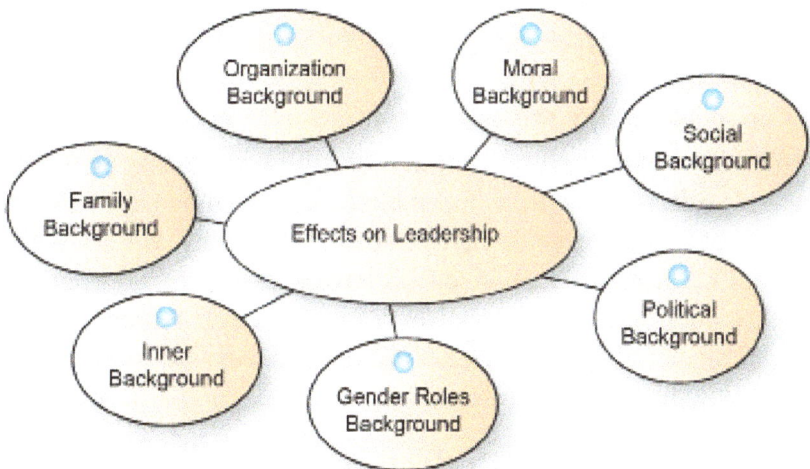

Fig. 3

Theme Two: *Leadership of Generation X women in Nigeria is an emerging trend.*

The general theme from this question was that leadership of Generation X women in Nigeria is seen as an emerging trend. While many in the Generation X group respect culture, and understand their roles in the family and society, their thinking is influenced by knowledge of worldviews and pop culture and the fast-paced, flat business environment. Many believe that with better knowledge, women can use education as a tool in fighting oppression and a correlation to their leadership style. The more knowledge and education, the better a Generation X woman can be assertive in opinions to speak her mind, especially to peers, subordinates and previous generations. Some of the responses from participants are below:

Respondent 009: "Having acquired good education, I feel thoroughly empowered to take on any task, knowing that, irrespective of the task's level of complexity, a little more research will enable me to overcome whatever obstacles are presented."

Respondent 012: "Older women have had more life experiences in terms of marriage, motherhood and all that goes with it. Considering this, they find it a lot easier (if they have adequate education and development) to lead out there in public. However, one's personality also affects leadership styles. Not all women in leadership can be rational or lead effectively. Women, first of all, need to be able to identify their areas of strength and know where they would function best."

Respondent 013: "My educational experience exposed me to styles of leadership I would not have considered as a woman, but have felt empowered to utilize."

Respondent 015: "I think that female leadership in Nigeria is fast gaining ground and, without a doubt, has great potential to have great positive impact on national life. As women are known to be natural managers, they no doubt pass on this skill to the workplace. Many Generation X women in Nigeria today have house staff who they have delegated their domestic chores to so they will have no problem managing the office front."

Respondent 018: "It is bending towards accepting the western world character—from fashion down to attitude. The family culture is gradually loosing grip on this generation. While this 'contemporary' way of life may seem easy, it also comes with its problems. First of all, it has no ground and no backing in our culture. Therefore, it is a transforming culture that needs and asks for attention."

Respondent 019: "I believe this varies from one ethnic group to the next. Being that I am a Yoruba, I feel that Yoruba women do not reply to institutionalized authority. In my opinion, the Generation X woman group that I belong to relies on recognized power, guiding their family away from danger and poverty. They strive to be in the position of authority."

Respondent 024: "Nigerian women worked hard to come this far, producing senators, bank managers and policy makers. At a point women controlled the country's economic team, and that was when Nigeria received debt relief owing to the leadership of Dr. Ngozi Okonjo-Iweala. Most of the women who have made an impact have fathers who believed in girl education. The conservative fathers don't send girl children to school and hardly select their daughters when opportunities like scholarships come up."

Respondent 026: "Culture is constant but it really does not exert power in my organization. There are business principles and strategies that must be applied for a successful biz lest we forget education, experience and so on. But culture should not be exerted in the business dynamics at all; it would be disorienting and confusing to the members of that organization."

Respondent 028: "First, the family one comes from tends to shape the kind of leadership one will eventually form. For instance, most normal firstborns tend to be 'natural leaders,' because they were often in charge of their younger siblings growing up. Also, these children were constantly reminded that 'someone was looking up to them,' so they naturally evolved as leaders. Now culturally, most traditional cultures in Nigeria do allow women to be in leadership except in the Muslim north, where men are still chauvinist. In fact, I must say that women featured more prominently in leadership roles in the pre-colonial days in Yoruba land than they did during the colonial period. A lot of damage was actually done to women's rights during the time of foreign intervention. For instance, all kings had a woman on their council, who was called the 'Iyalode' and she was usually a VERY powerful woman... However, after the colonial period ended, and we started to use foreign styles of leadership, men became more disrespectful towards women, and there has been a lot of imbalance since in the way women are viewed in leadership in Africa."

Primary Research Question Three: *How do Generation X women in positions of power in Nigeria view and use power within the organization?*

The intent of this question was to understand from participants' perspectives what they believed they could accomplish in the organization with their status in a leadership position. This question also sought to understand the view and perspectives of Generation X women in positions of power in Nigeria and how they relate their leadership styles to their environment. The following sub-themes emerged as shown in Figure 4:

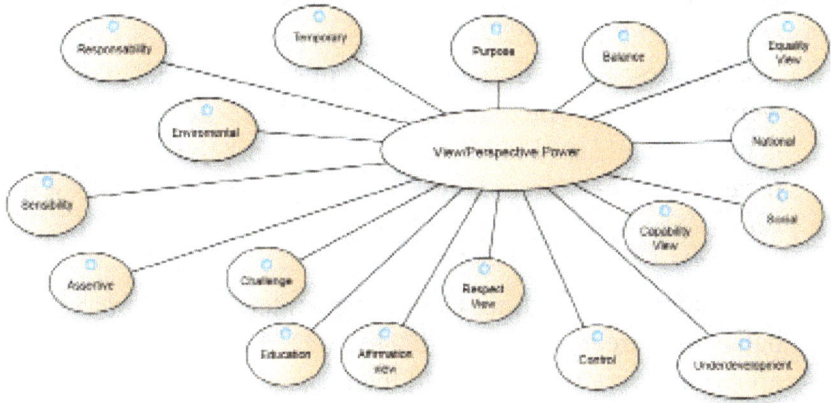

Fig. 4

Theme Three: *Differences in leadership styles of Generation X women*

The general theme from this research question was that the leadership style characteristics of Generation X women are used as tools of empowerment and not as an ascribed or prescribed role of women in the society. They believe that the rules or organizational culture come first, which assists them in determining their leadership styles. Some of the responses from participants are below:

Respondent 003: "Most women in the Generation X group seem to be ignoring the family aspect of their responsibilities, unlike most of the women that precede us. The society seems to have taken up a lot of the work most women should be doing at home, and that is why the level of societal and moral decadence is on the increase. The women of the past seem to have given their best shot to both and really fared better."

Respondent 004: "The major difference between the leadership styles is that the Generation X leaders are more willing to take risks in management and readily seek advancements and changes happening in the world around them."

Respondent 009: "I reckon the predecessors approached leadership from the 'maternal' angle. They sought to run organizations like families. They exhibited greater tolerance for defaulters and were less likely to mete out discipline. The Generation X leader is more professional minded, and seeks more to drive the organization and her career forward, many times irrespective of the stance of others."

Respondent 013: "I think Gen X women feel less pressure about balancing career and family due to more choices. Gen X women are probably more empowered than past generations."

Respondent 019: "The preceding generation is called baby boomers. They are the largest generational demographic in history. Based on their leadership role, they established careers and earned money to spend on their families more than any other generation. This generation makes 90 percent of their household purchasing decisions, which is also considered as 'power.' Generation X women make the same income and sometimes more than their spouses. Women in the Generation X group are more independent, and sometimes cannot be compared to the baby boomers."

Respondent 021: "The main difference for me is as Generation X women, we were taught to believe in ourselves and know that we can achieve and be anything we want to as long as we worked hard. The women that preceded us had the mentality that the men are supposed to be in charge, and a woman's job is to take care of the house and raise kids."

Respondent 028: "Educationally, it gives me more confidence to lead because I know what I'm talking about. I think a leader's job is difficult if you are 'less' than the people you are leading. Economics doesn't figure into it much. But I must say that having a better income has allowed me to buy better working clothes. And I've noticed that any time I'm dressed up, I feel more 'in charge.' So I always wear a suit (or equivalent)."

Respondent 029: "Women in the Generation X group are more enlightened, thus, are standing up more for their rights. They are moving higher on the achievement ladder. Generation X women are more aggressive and assertive in their leadership roles."

Respondent 030: "Tolerance, ambition, sentiments, transformation, growth--these are major factors that come between these categories of women leaders. The pattern of the new generation woman is to undermine any setback and forge ahead."

Data Triangulation

Triangulation is a method used in qualitative research to corroborate multiple sources of information or themes. Triangulation was used throughout the follow-up interviews and coding process to ensure the authenticity and validity of the data collection. It also ensured that standards of authenticity were met. Data was collected to explore themes and theories provided by the research (Creswell, 2005). Creswell pointed out that triangulation permits research participants an opportunity to provide any clarifying answers to research questions at the conclusion of the interviews, ensuring the accuracy of data and participant responses. The data analysis permitted developing theories and patterns provided by the perceptions and experiences of the research participants (Creswell).

Triangulation is a means of achieving validity and is also used to confirm and complete the research (Casey & Murphy, 2009). It assists the researcher in gaining a holistic view of the phenomenon understudy and adds to the depth and breadth of understanding of the research (Fenech-Adami, 2005). Data for the current study was triangulated after the transcribed information from the questionnaires was confirmed by the participants for authenticity. This allowed the questionnaires to be completed for reliability and validity based on additional feedback from the survey interview participants.

Descriptive Outcomes

The results of the descriptive outcomes below are based on answers to the survey questionnaires that were derived from the primary research questions and the themes above. The descriptions summarize participants' perceptions and their day-to-day lived experiences as women belonging to the Generation X group in positions of power in their organizations and businesses in Nigeria. The interview descriptions and the corresponding lived experiences provide the general analysis of the data as summarized.

Interview Question 1: Obstacles Encountered

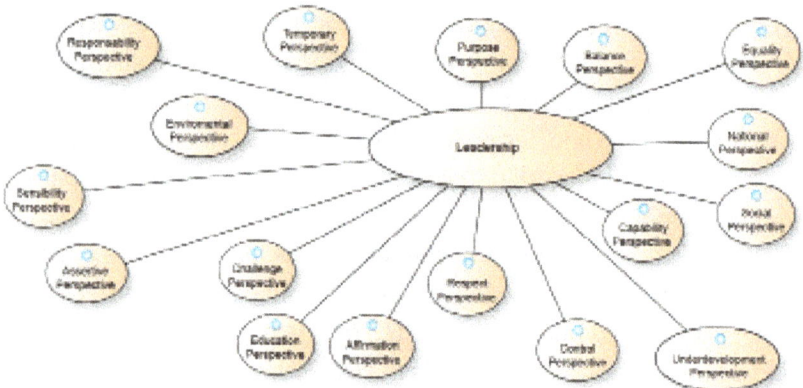

Fig. 5

When asked what the obstacles encountered by women in positions of power were, some of the responses were that national and cultural challenges of the prescribed traditional role of women in Nigeria were obstacles they encountered in their day-to-day leadership experience. Affirmation and the general need for women to work harder to advance to the same or higher level of leadership position as men was an obstacle to the leadership of Generation X women. Sometimes, Generation X women have to work twice as hard as the previous generation due to their young age to counter some of the obstacles in their day-to-day leadership.

Another obstacle some of the participants have encountered were in the area of access to financial markets and funding for some of their programs, projects, and businesses. Participants were stable financially on the job, but most of the female entrepreneurs disclosed that it was difficult for them to obtain loans and financial support from banks. Sometimes, they had to co-sign with their husbands or a male representative from their family. Other answers included the approval of others about the leader's knowledge, skills, recognition, and personal conviction; going the extra mile to be taken seriously; understanding the environment and political landscape at work; and using knowledge to manage expectations and communicate effectively.

Many women in Nigeria are not financially empowered given that men control the major means of production. Males and those who own the means of production and access to financial institutions are not in a hurry to empower the women and therefore, continue to set obstacles in their way.

Other obstacles facing Generation X women in positions of power include the fast-paced flat business environment, sexual harassment, organizational or business size, disciplinary challenges of the older generation of both male and female, maternity leave allowance, global trends, and the rapidly changing worldview (pop-culture). Generation X women in positions of power also struggle with the general view of organizational leadership across different cultures that may be different in some organizations and business settings in Nigeria. Finally, several of the participants responded that Generation X women in positions of power feel that they have to constantly measure up to other people's views of management, and leadership perspectives.

Interview Question 2: Perspective of Power

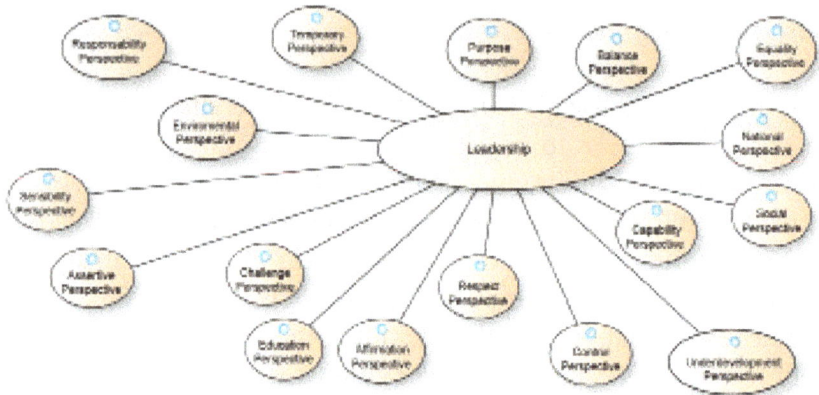

Fig. 6

When asked what their views of power were as women in positions of power, respondents stated that they desired the ability to openly display power based on certain cultural factors and depending on the environment or region. Some of the answers that emerged were that power was gaining the approval of others about the leader's knowledge, skills, recognition, personal conviction, going the extra mile to be taken seriously, understanding the environment and political landscape at work, and using the knowledge to manage expectations and communicate effectively. Participants disclosed that responsibility, integrity, the ability to control, act, and lead positively, and the opportunity to lead, make rules, and punish rightly within the organization were important aspects of power.

Interview Question 3: Treatment by Peers and Subordinates

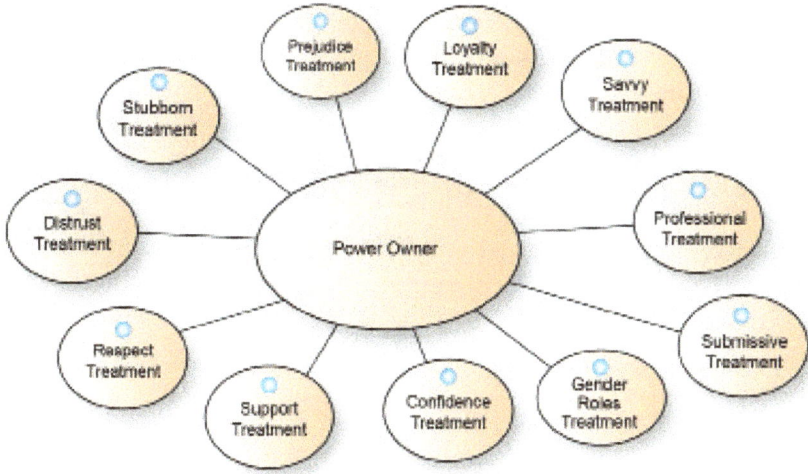

Fig. 7

When asked how women in leadership positions were treated by subordinates (both men and women), some of the responses were that women were skeptical, confrontational and judgmental. Men are divided; some are very loyal, respectful, supportive, cooperative and very helpful. Some respondents answered that men are difficult, rude and impossible, and many believed that women in the Generation X age group were too young and inexperienced. Other respondents believed that power is class-based and not influenced by age or experience. Some women had good, quality access to education, finances, and social connections, which enhanced their ascension to leadership positions and generated resentment among some of their colleagues.

Interview Question 4: Asset of the Use of Power

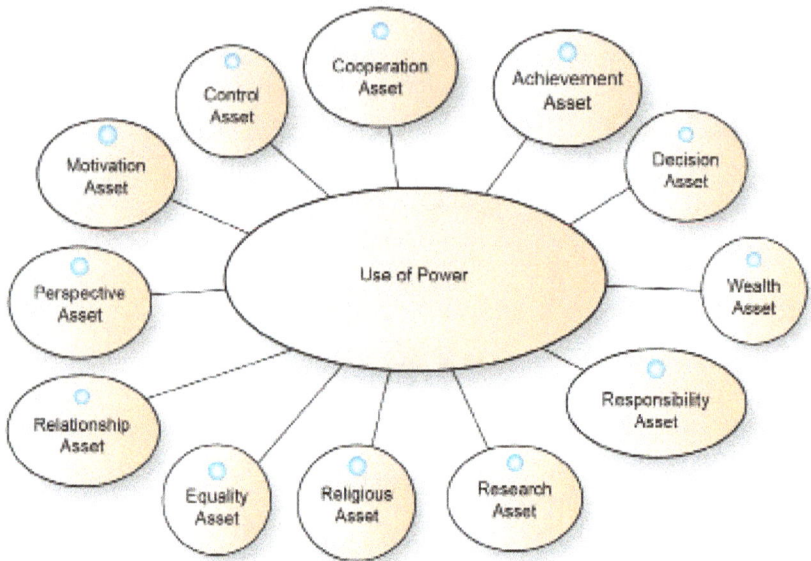

Fig. 8

When asked to describe an asset of power, some of the responses were that power is viewed as an achievement that allows discipline, control, reliability, and the ability to achieve results and get the job done. Power asset provides an opportunity for participants to show-case their talents, skills, professionalism, hard work and dedication. The ability to take responsibility, build trust in relationships with their supervisors and subordinates, and command respect is an asset of power. This asset of power encourages cooperation and support as well as the opportunity to motivate subordinates for staff devel-opment and make a difference in the lives of others in the society. Power as an asset allows for clearer goals to be achieved through well-thought decision-making processes and active listening. This enables some of the participants to establish a vision and long-term goals, problem solve, have self-confidence and in–depth knowledge of business and organizational environment and the ability to gener-ate returns for stakeholders.

Interview Question 5: Generation X and Power

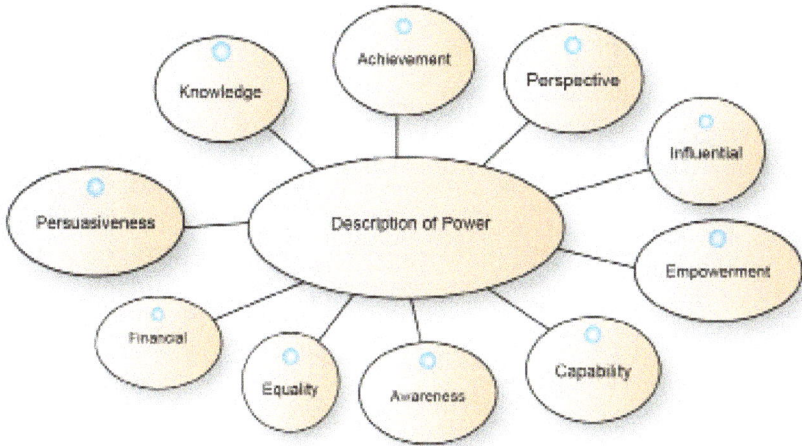

Fig. 9

Many of the respondents believed that the ability to be in a position of power while in a younger age group was a great achievement. Several of the respondents answered that the ability to be able to meet deliverables within the organization, influence others from a different and diverse perspective, be financially stable, and have self–confidence and independence meant power. The opportunity to have the knowledge to be empowered in different aspects of Nigerian life, especially being exposed to new technologies, is a power that Generation X possesses. Others answered living in a diverse and multi-cultural society where different ethnicities, religions, and languages are present has given them power to communicate in the Nigerian society. The power of Generation X was also viewed as the breaking of some cultural norms and social barriers that relegated women to the background.

Interview Question 6: Role of National and Family Culture on Power

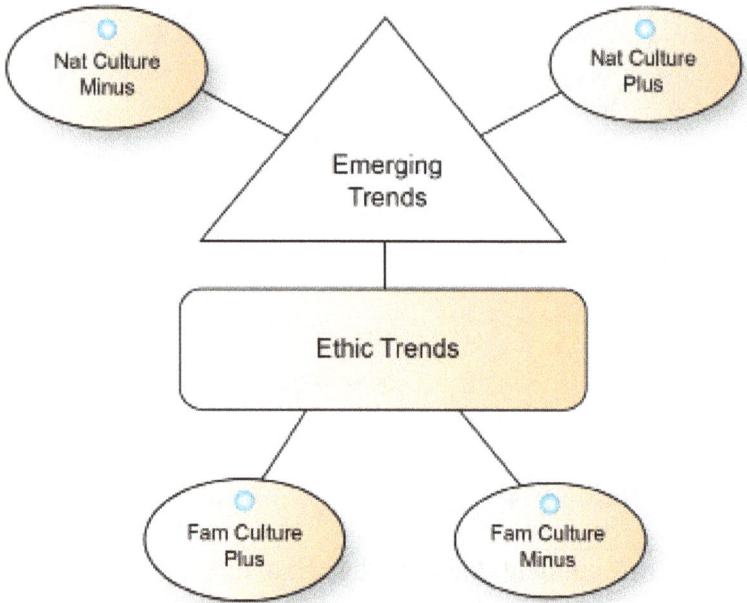

Fig. 10

When asked to describe what the role of both the national and family culture of Nigeria was on the leadership styles of women belonging to the Generation X group, many of the participants responded both positively and negatively to this question. Out of the 15 open-ended questions asked, question six was the richest in analysis with diverse perspectives from the participants. One respondent answered that national and family culture is an emerging trend when describing Generation X, because many people still expect women to submit to men, even when those women are more qualified. Another participant answered that the natural tendency of Nigeria's culture was to assign family roles to women. This culture is weakening as more and more women continue to succeed in the corporate, political and business worlds. Many of the respondents believed that contrary to the common opinion that culture does not permit women to be leaders, both family and national culture can be used as a tool to help nurture the great potentials in women.

For instance, culture lays emphasis on the woman as a homemaker and by experience, the better homemakers are better leaders. The national and family cultures in Nigeria are rapidly changing and now find more women in management and leadership roles. This has become especially true since Nigeria returned to democratic rule in 1999, and more women have been involved in politics and elected or appointed to serve in government and lead major corporations in the country. Their successes have marked a dynamic and transitional shift, given the number of young women that have continued to climb the economic and leadership ladder.

From many participants' points-of-view, cultural perceptions in Nigeria affect the leadership role of women because Nigerian culture does not easily embrace the concept of women holding leadership positions in the society. Men are perceived as the head of the family even where, as is the case these days, women are the bread winners. The Nigerian culture, in one respondent's view, has grossly hampered the development of women. Less importance is attached to the birth and development of female children, especially in the respondent's community. Ignorance and lack of extensive exposure have limited the potential of women leaders in Nigeria. "Women need more education, more exposure, and more development so as to boost their self–esteem." Another respondent doubted that the Nigerian culture fully believes and accepts what it professes.

In Nigeria, the national culture is, at least on the surface, supportive of women in leadership positions, and at the family level, it varies. There is the assumption that a woman in leadership ceases to be womanly. For instance, she loses all sense of femininity and womanliness, and so she is perceived as not fit for marriage. This trend in the Generation X group has seen a high number of professional women being unmarried. The fact that Nigeria operates a highly familial culture results in added pressure on the professional woman for marriage and children from the family circle.

Finally, when asked what role the national and family culture has played on the leadership styles of Generation X women in Nigeria, many of the respondents stated that in terms of education and knowledge, Generation X women needed to travel far and wide to meet other women in leadership positions—especially those in higher leadership positions. An educated woman makes a whole lot of difference as a mother, a mentor, a leader and a counselor.

Interview Question 7: Cultural Values when Exercising Power

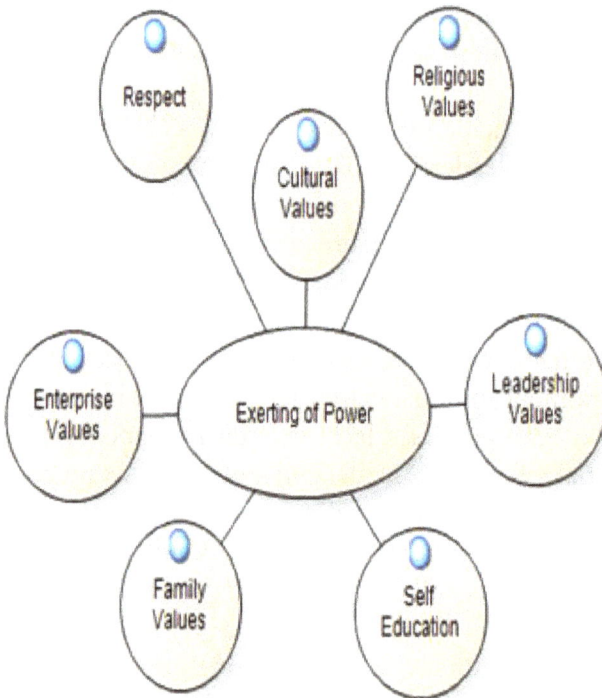

Fig. 11

When asked if respondents considered their cultural values when exerting power within the organization, the following were some of the patterns that emerged. Some of the participants responded by saying "yes," especially when it came to addressing older generations of Nigerians whether at work, at home, or in social situations, because the Nigerian culture values and respects the older generations. One participant responded that as a leader, she had to defer to those in higher positions regardless of their cultural values, respect others' opinions, listen to the wishes and aspirations of subordinates, and carry everyone along, particularly the men-folk who did not believe in the abilities of a female leader. Some responded that generally, one huge problem is that men feel that Generation X women in positions of power are trying to measure up to them.

Several of the respondents replied that "No," they did not consider their cultural values when exercising power within the organization, especially in a target driven organization where they needed to drive their subordinates regardless of their gender. One respondent explained that the Nigerian culture gives the utmost regard to those who are older. "Good as it sounds, it creates obstacles in the workplace when there is a need to delegate tasks and address or discipline an older member of staff." Another participant answered that she did not consider her cultural values. As a Nigerian woman, it came naturally, though it sometimes hindered the fast flow and regulations of a business. A different participant answered that she did not consider cultural values in leadership, because it did not add to organizational growth. The participant further went on to say that leaders who want growth in their organizations have to play by the rules and that they do need to be firm in decision-making that they believe is the way forward. "Workplace rules are sacrosanct. The office is not a village market square, but a cooperate organization from which investors expect a return on investment. But they do treat elders with respect."

Interview Question 8: Differences in Leadership of the Previous Generation

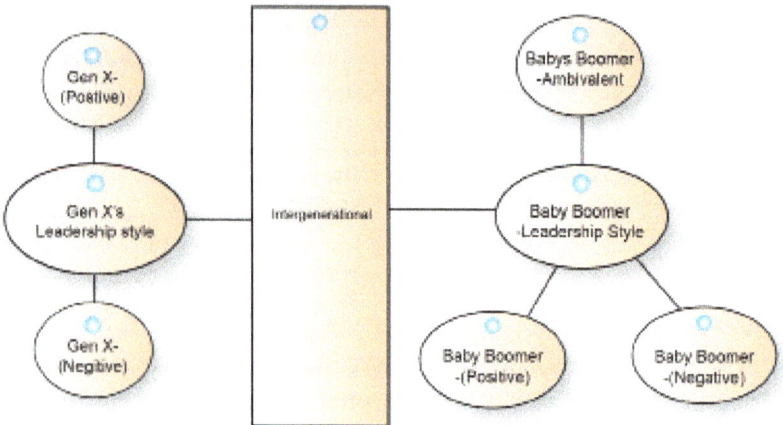

Fig. 12

When asked what the differences in leadership between the Generation X women in positions of power were compared to previous generations, such as the baby boomer generation of women leaders, many of the respondents answered that the previous generations were always respectful, laid back, and intimidated because of their family and national background and the role that women played in the society as nurturers and homemakers. Additionally, this generation was considered to be more submissive, tolerant, and sentimental, from a maternal angle. They were not as independent as Generation X women. One respondent answered that older women have had more life experiences regarding marriage, motherhood and all that went with it. Considering this, they found it a lot easier (if they had adequate education and professional development) to lead in public.

In describing the leadership styles of Generation X women, many of the participants responded that Generation X women are more vocal, bold, and confident. They have a higher exposure to others in the environment and have a diversified world view. They have higher levels of education at younger ages than the previous generation. Generation X women are perceived to take more risks, to readily seek advancements, to be more informed and professionally minded, to seek to drive their organizational goals, and to move their careers forward irrespective of the stances of others.

The glass ceiling seems to have been broken down a lot more in the Generation X group than in the previous baby boomer group, said one respondent. With technological advancements, globalization and knowledge management, Generation X women in leadership are thought to be more audacious, have less pressure about balancing their familial duties with their careers, and have more choices than the previous generation. Some respondents answered that even though Generation X women are more confident in their approach to leadership, the leadership styles of women depend on their knowledge, their professional sectors, and their organization's culture, and not necessarily on their generation. The pattern of the new generation woman is to undermine any setback and forge ahead, more than the previous generation of women leaders.

Interview Question 9: Treatment by Previous Generations

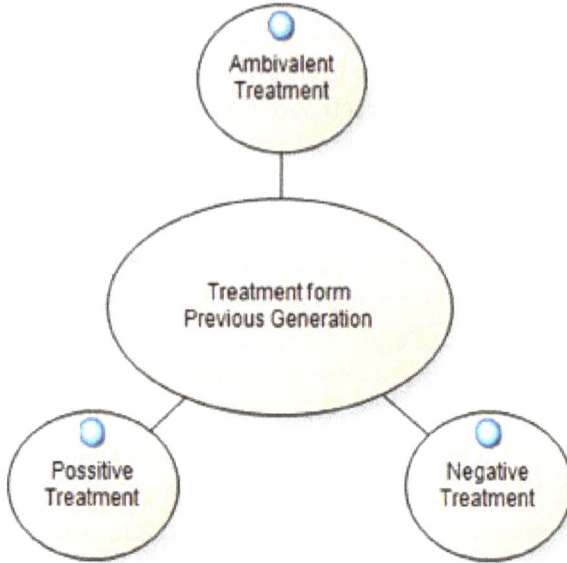

Fig. 13

When asked how the previous generation of women leaders, especially those in the baby boomer generation treated women of Generation X in positions of power, many of the respondents answered that most preceding generations of women leaders treated women in the Generation X group as a group that seemed to ignore the familial aspect of their responsibilities. The society seems to have taken up a lot of the work most women should be doing at home, and that is why the level of societal and moral decadence is on the increase. Generation X women are stricter and firmer than preceding generations. Some replied that the previous generation treated them with envy and condescension because they were more independent and had more opportunities at younger ages than the preceding generation. "They tend to look down on younger women leaders due to their age and believe that younger women do not have the experience."

Many of the respondents answered that they have had good experiences with preceding generations, because they have more life experiences, and they are supportive, encouraging, and mostly treat the Generation X women with respect. However, some see Generation X women in positions of leadership as competition and being in a hurry to take over a man's world. For the most part, baby boomers have served as mentors and been supportive to Generation X women. They view this generation more from the angle of pity, and not respect. Maybe rightly so, they believe the priorities of Generation X are muddled up. For them, the quest and desire for the family will always eventually resurface, and they believed that the Generation X group is putting off starting a family a little too late, and they might regret it later.

Interview Question 10: Effects of Demographics on View of Power

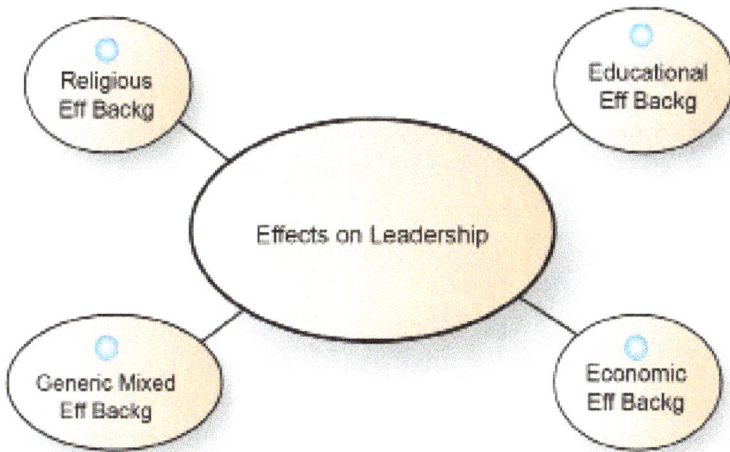

Fig. 14

When asked about the role of participants' demographics and their effects on their views of power, many answered that their educational, economic, and religious backgrounds have had positive effects on their leadership styles and views of power. One respondent answered that her present demographics had given her the power to realize that she could achieve whatever she set her mind to achieve, as long as she stayed hardworking, honest, and trustworthy. Another responded that in a lot of ways, her "religious and economic background kept her humble and taught her not to abuse power."

Several of the respondents answered that good finances gave them more confidence and power to be able to afford courses and training on leadership. Another responded that coming from a relatively humble background economically, she witnessed the amount of regard power bestows on a person. "The level of power a person wields determines where he or she speaks, and who listens to them. It determines those who seek to do business with them, and the amount of contribution and effect they can have on their community."

Another respondent said that her economic background made her comfortable to perform her leadership role without fear or favor, knowing that in the worst case scenario, if she lost her job for challenging a superior, she would not starve or die of poverty. These women's economic backgrounds enabled many of them to give back to society and motivated them to encourage subordinates to achieve economic independence.

One respondent answered that her education gave her the power she needed to know and understand business from all aspects of the books. Another replied that she felt the path that she chose in her level of education paved the way for a good career, and that she had better opportunities than many women in her ethnic and age groups. One respondent mentioned that education impacted her view of power positively, as she could influence the lives of many people who perceived her as a role model and aspired to get an education. Another respondent answered that their educational experience exposed them to different styles of leadership that she would not have considered as a woman because of her cultural background, but now felt empowered to utilize.

On religious background, several of the respondents answered that religion taught them to treat everyone equally, respectfully, and fairly when delegating responsibilities and instituting religious actions. Religion influenced participants' backgrounds, making them believe that everyone should be treated with respect and that positive motivation provided results beyond intimidation and bullying in an organization. According to one respondent, religion greatly influenced her view on power because she believed that teachings of servant-hood influenced her to be more of a participatory rather than a dictatorial leader. "Portraying good work ethics is something that gets people far in their career, and in their view and use of power, which enables them to have the ability to influence and to lead by example."

Interview Question 11: Leadership and Decision-Making Styles

Hofstede (1980) defined culture as the collective programming of the mind that distinguishes the members of a group from another. Hofstede (1980, 1991, 1994, and 2001) developed a cultural dimension model based on a research study done in 67 countries. In the study, he discussed the influence of culture on individual behavior. Hofstede identified five dimensions: (a) Power distance, (b) Individualism/collectivism, (c) Masculinity/femininity, (d) Uncertainty avoidance, (e) Long-term/short-term orientation. Participants for this study were asked to select an attribute of their leadership and decision-making style in Research Question 11. Since respondents were asked to check a box signifying their leadership and decision–making style choice, there were no written expressions on this question. Figures 15, 16, and 17 show percentages of the participants in relation to the leadership and decision-making styles selected.

Leadership & Decision Making Style

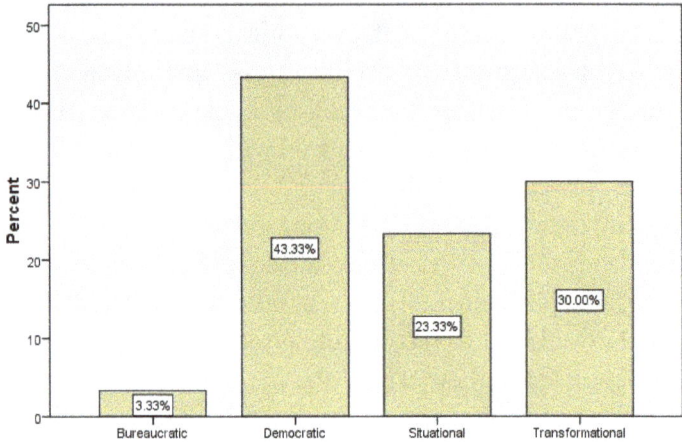

Leadership & Decision-Making Style
Fig. 15

Figure 15 depicts the regions of the respondents and their leadership and decision-making styles. Out of the 30 participants, one respondent utilized the bureaucratic method of leadership, 13 of the respondents utilized the democratic styles of leadership. Seven of the respondents used the situational styles of leadership while nine of them participants utilized the transformational style of leadership. None of the 30 participants selected the autocratic or laissez–faire styles of leadership.

Bar Chart

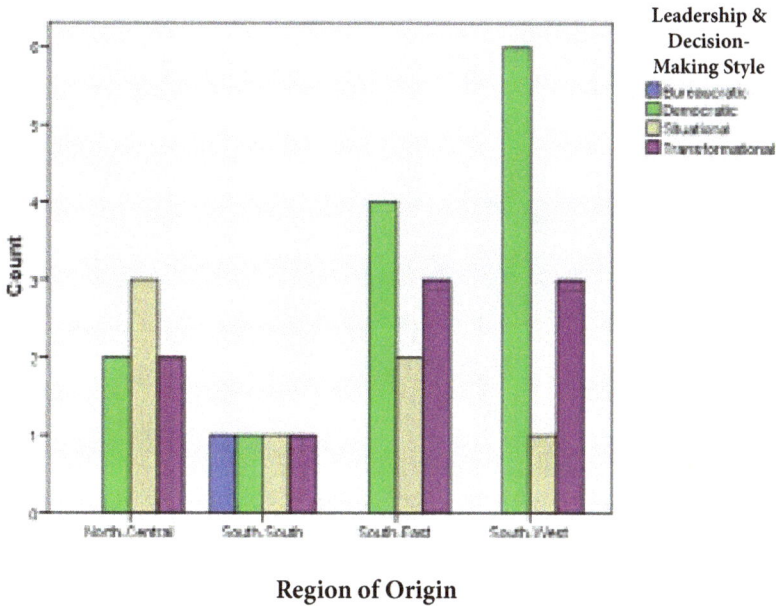

Region of Origin

Fig. 16

The results based on the age ranges of participants were as follows. Between the ages of 30 to 34, five of them selected the democratic style, 3 of them selected the situational style. The other five selected the transformational style of leadership while none of the participants between the ages of 30 to 34 selected the autocratic or bureaucratic styles of leadership. Out of the 10 participants between the ages of 35 to 39, one selected the bureaucratic style, three selected the democratic style, and four selected the situational style and two selected the transformational style. Of the two participants between the ages of 40 to 44, none selected the bureaucratic, situational, or transformational styles of leadership, but they both selected the democratic style of leadership. Out of the five participants between the ages of 45 and over, none selected the bureaucratic or situational styles of leadership but three of them selected the democratic style while the other two selected the transformational style of leadership.

Bar Chart

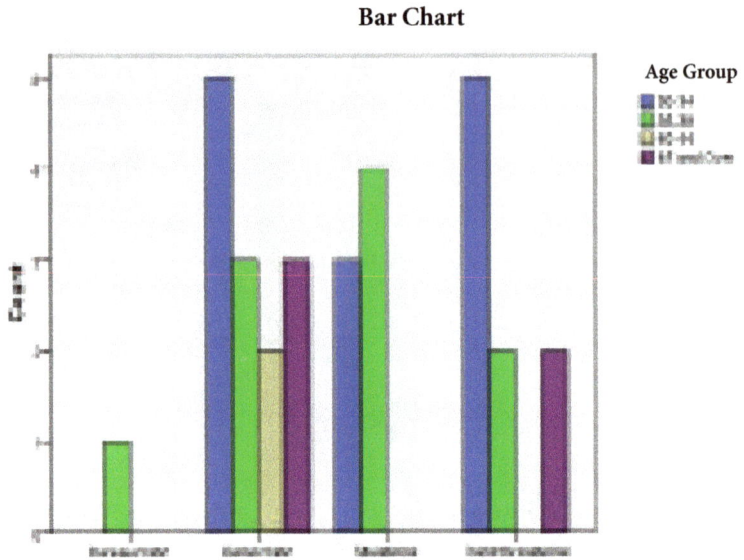

Fig. 17   Leadership & Decision Making Style

Interview Question 12: Reasons for Selecting Leadership Style

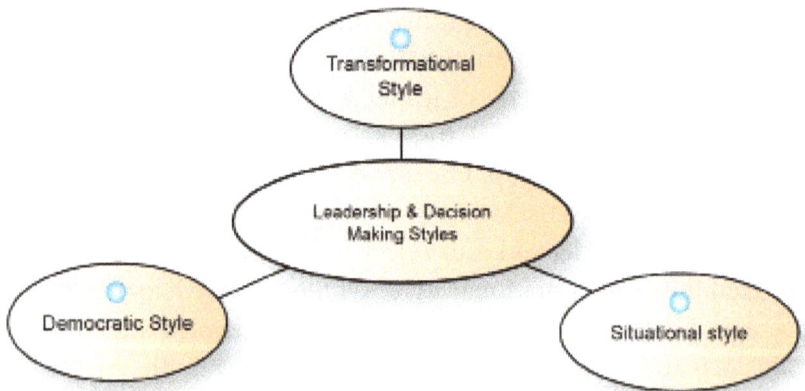

Fig. 18

Democratic Style

In a democratic workplace, a leader has to exhibit vision, adjust to present circumstances, and make decisions that are legally allowed to meet the organizational mission, vision and objectives. The democratic approach to leadership was selected most by the research participants because of the team building aspect and ability to be inclusive and understand others. They found these qualities in a leadership style to be important asset because of the various cultural backgrounds and ethnic groups present in the Nigerian society.

Some respondents answered that this approach provided subordinates with a sense of belonging and feeling of responsibility, because they took part in the decision-making processes of the company. They felt committed to the job when they knew that someone was not just forcing the decisions on them. The democratic approach to leadership was selected most by the research participants because of its team building aspect and ability to be inclusive and understand others. They found these qualities in a leadership style to be important asset because of the various cultural backgrounds and ethnic groups present in the Nigerian society. Some respondents answered that this approach provided subordinates with a sense of belonging and feeling of responsibility, because they took part in the decision-making processes of the company. They felt committed to the job when they knew that someone was not just forcing the decisions on them.

Subordinates have ownership spirit and more commitment when they are included as part of the team. They have the freedom to come up with views on subjects and suggestions without feeling that they are being judged due to their level within the organization, because their leaders believe every experience is important. Each person has something to bring to the table. People have strengths and weaknesses. Democratic leaders allow subordinates and team members to make contributions and suggest ways of achieving goals, because while carrying out assignments, leaders can then meet different people that have different approaches to problem-solving. One can only tap into other people's knowledge bases when one lets them know that their contributions, ideas, and suggestions are important to the organization.

One person answered that the democratic leadership style approach got the full cooperation of everyone in getting the job done on time. This respondent selected this style of leadership because she believed that the ability to understand that working with different personalities from diverse backgrounds, who speak, behave, and reason differently from her, was a potential asset to her organization.

This approach assists in making immense contributions in realizing organizational goals, because everyone has something to offer in a collective and all-inclusive environment. Team members can proffer solutions in problem areas if needed, when leaders are at a loss. Exhibiting this leadership style approach notwithstanding, the leader is still able to apply disciplinary measures if need be, without fear or favor, so everyone is on the same page.

The democratic method allowed one respondent to learn constantly. She believed that just because she was in a position of power did not mean that her subordinates could not teach her something new. By asking questions and engaging subordinates and colleagues in the decision-making process, different perspectives came to the surface and provided a richer work environment. As a team player, she said that "leaders need the support of their subordinates otherwise, the job will not be done, as they are not capable of performing the job alone."

"The need to respect the ideas of others within a team of people means the ability to collaborate and communicate feedback before a final decision can be made about anything we do in the organization, as every member of the team has valuable input. Two good heads are better than one," responded another participant. The staff is employed based on different competencies so that they have to work as a team. "Nobody knows it all and allowing others to make input makes us

Situational Style

Some participants selected the situational style of leadership based on their work with people of different educational and social backgrounds and those with different needs; therefore, changing their leadership styles from time to time was a perfect choice. One participant responded that in her place of business, customers were never sure until the last minute, so one needed to go with the flow and try to adapt to the customers' requests, because her organization believed that the customers were always right. Adapting to the changing environmental and business needs of stakeholders allowed many of the participants to change from one leadership style to the other. The complex and dynamic nature of another participant's job, she had to adapt to changing needs and people in the organization, so she chose the situational style of leadership. Flexibility was another reason some of the participants selected the situational style of leadership.

Many respondents believed that they worked better with bosses who were flexible and considerate of their needs. Therefore, they, in turn, have been considerate and flexible towards the needs of their subordinates. By actively listening to what staff has to say, one can determine what the mood in the organizational environment is. One participant believed that if one went a particular way, there would be no room for growth. As a leader, one has to delegate duties to the right people and lead by example. People are different, and one is bound to see new things. Therefore, one has to adapt or change things as they come. One respondent answered that "no man is an island, so you need to obtain other people's ideas to function as a leader and give enough room for change in the organizational by being flexible."

Transformational Style

The transformational leadership style was the most sustainable, in some of the respondents' views. They engaged this style not only because it got the job done in the immediate, but also because it changed people, thereby effecting a lasting change in lives. It is important to mentor and inspire subordinates so as to get them to deliver optimally and more effectively. Leading by example, encouraging, motivating, inspiring, and showing personal examples through stories were some of the reasons respondents selected the transformational leadership style. Teamwork in a target and goal-driven organization was important to many of the participants. Therefore, they ensured that their team members clearly understood the goals. Together they developed and implemented strategies to achieve those goals. Some of these respondents were also responsible for ensuring that all limitations toward meeting those goals were resolved within the organization.

Interview Question 13: Day-to-Day Challenges

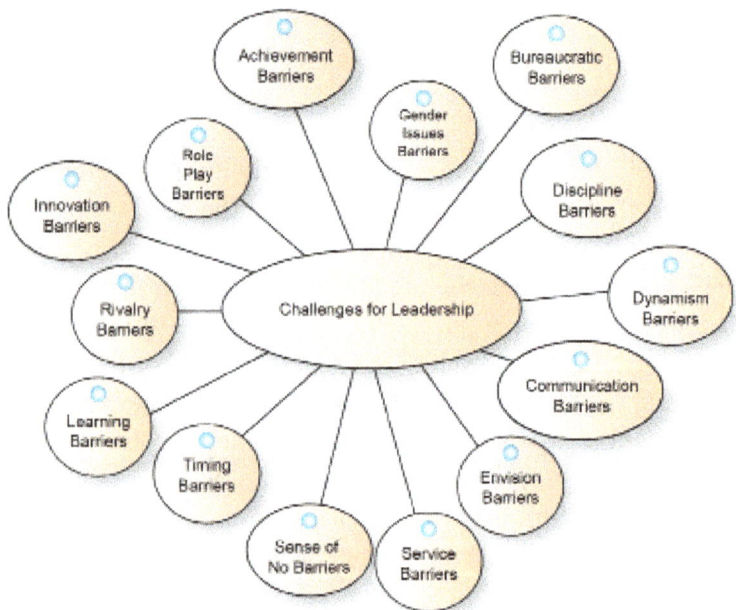

Fig. 19

Many of the respondents viewed the day-to-day challenges of their selected leadership styles in terms of achievement barriers, innovative challenges, discipline, communication, and timing difficulties. They needed to prove they were capable of doing the job by providing a different perspective to subordinates on a regular basis in order to achieve set organizational goals. Excessive scrutiny and unnecessary criticism from superiors are some of the day-to-day challenges Generation X women in positions of power face on the job. Other day-to-day challenges of expressing some of the participant's leadership style were bureaucratic bottlenecks, lack of confidence from some supervisors, communication barriers, and the need to develop new skills to motivate subordinates. Additional challenges included managers not being responsive enough to Generation X women in positions of power, or staff members not willing to conduct business with integrity.

One respondent answered that enforcing rules and taking disciplinary action against older or male subordinates posed several challenges, as those subordinates had difficulty accepting direction from women in a leadership role, especially from someone from the Generation X group. "People still view the African woman as incapable of making rational decisions and fail to promote or encourage her to move further in her career."

The fact that there were more baby boomers from various ethnic backgrounds within one respondent's organization than members from any other generation meant that there were constant changes in policy, procedures, and processes. This frequent change in policy posed a challenge or rivalry, because others had to adhere to everyday changes and decisions. Another day-to-day challenge for participants was the poor time management of some staff members who delayed everyone's opinion and decision-making because they did not keep to deadlines, schedules or timelines.

Some of the respondents faced more challenges dealing with other women. For example, they had to deal with married women who women. For example, they had to deal with married women who gave excuses about their inability to perform their duties because of their family issues. The fact that there were more baby boomers from various ethnic backgrounds within one respondent's organization than members from any other generation, meant that there were constant changes in policy, procedures, and processes. This frequent change in policy posed a challenge or rivalry, because others had to adhere to everyday changes and decisions. Another day-to-day challenge for participants was the poor time management of some staff members who delayed everyone's opinion and decision-making because they did not keep to deadlines, schedules or timelines.

Interview Question 14: Role of Societal Culture on Leadership Style

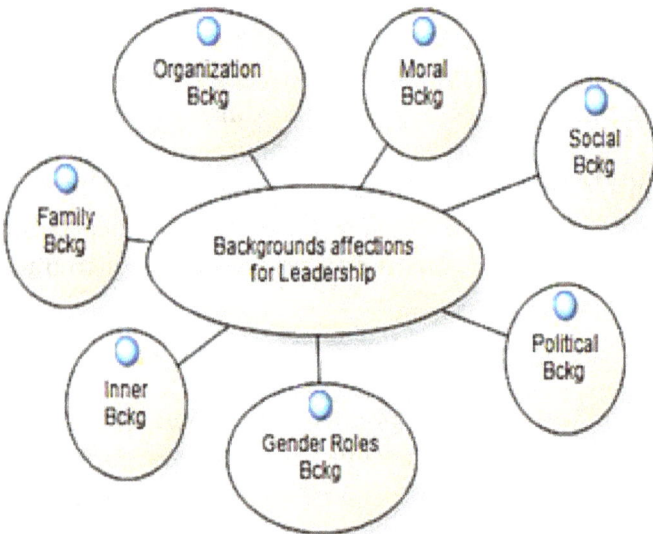

Fig. 20

Many respondents answered positively that the supportive family background, learned family values, and moral support boosted their self-esteem and contributed immensely to their current leadership positions. Societal culture has assisted many women in positions of power to learn to be good leaders. Participants believed that one had to earn one's position in society, whether in the family, society, or the organization. Some respondents also believed that "one has to be a good follower before they can be a good leader." Society expects women to be less corrupt and maintain high moral standards in a largely corrupt setup. Initially, one respondent was more considerate about cultural issues, such as considering the manner in which she spoke to elders. However, the reality of the work environment was that the workplace culture dictated her leadership style.

One respondent answered that her strong determination in giving out the best of her leadership position to her employer did not allow societal and national culture or family background to affect her leadership style and view of power. This respondent believed that their leadership style was impacted by her upbringing. Another respondent answered that Nigeria is a country where respect for elders is very important. "There is the need to say 'Sir' or 'Ma' to older subordinates and people in the society. It is gratifying to see the return of respect from the older generations of Nigerians when they see that someone in the Generation X group was able to attain the level of power and leadership that they hold in the organization."

Culture and family background enhanced the view of power and leadership style of one participant. She believed that "one should not let power get to one's head," but rather, use their power to "be a good role model." On the negative side, culture had affected the leadership styles of some participants tremendously because they had to always keep the family background, Nigerian culture, and their peers and societal views regarding how a woman should behave in mind before dictating or delegating tasks in the business environment. As much as women are crossing the cultural or societal barriers, it is still believed in some quarters that some positions cannot be held by women. Therefore, the role of national and family culture has both its positive and negative aspects in influencing the leadership styles of Generation X women in Nigeria.

Interview Question 15: Universal Style of Leadership

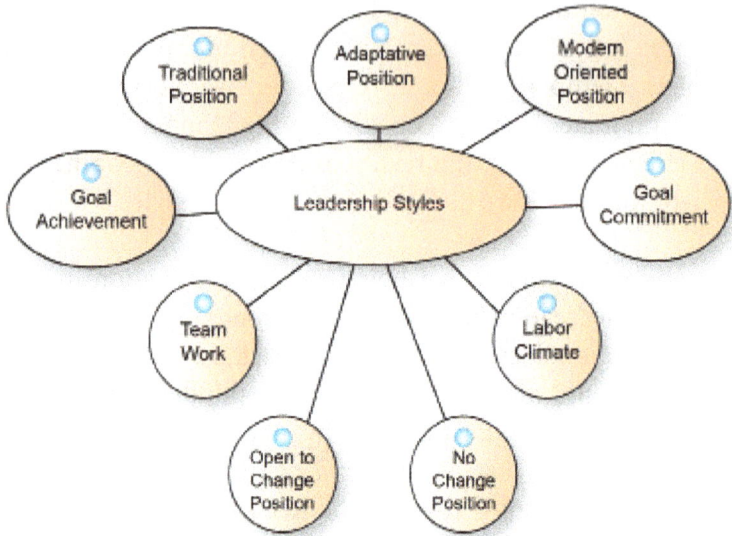

Fig. 21

When asked if respondents would consider changing their selected leadership styles and if so, which leadership styles they would select, many respondents answered that they were not interested in changing their selected styles of leadership due to adaptive reasons. They were not very comfortable conforming to the general mold of leadership. They preferred to work with what they were used to, and what worked for them to achieve the best results. Many believed that they were who they were and that their leadership style assisted them in the organization in reaching set goals and leading others to yield results. They believed that leading effectively may mean different things to different people. For some, it is whatever gets the job done. They push, coax, pamper, and sanction as needed, and not because someone said so.

Another reason some participants gave for why they would not change their current leadership style was goal achievement. Unless other leadership styles were bound to produce the necessary results and contribute differently to the goals of their organizations, some participants believed that they were satisfied with their selected leadership styles. Due to clear goal commitment in a democratic workplace, a leader has to exhibit vision, adjust to present circumstances, and make decisions that meet the organization's mission, vision, and objectives. "Some things are 'timeless principles' and changing them just makes society worse. For example, hard work brings rewards. That is a timeless principle that does not need fixing," responded one participant.

"From a 21st century modern perspective, many youthful leaders desire change in Nigeria," answered another respondent. "If they have to change their orientation to make things happen, then they will consider changing their selected leadership style." Two respondents who selected the situational style of leadership stated that they would have selected the democratic style due to the teamwork approach, if they were working with more educated staff and subordinates in their organization. But due to the region and the types of people that they worked with, the situational style of leadership suited their organizational cultures and social environments. Overall, many of the respondents would not have selected or utilized a different style of leadership even if it meant adhering to a universal style of organizational leadership in the 21st century due to some of the reasons that have been stated above.

Summary

Data analysis was presented using the Van Kaam (1994) methods and Creswell (2005) steps. Research triangulated was achieved when the researcher confirmed from respondents questionnaire answers for feedback and confirmation. This process completed the research triangulation for validity and reliability. It was determined that data saturation was established after several of the survey questionnaires produced the same patterns and themes needed for the study. More details regarding the descriptive outcomes can be found in the appendix section.

The role of culture on the leadership styles of women in leadership positions is seen as an emerging trend, where the younger generation of women is ascending the professional ladder faster. More women are earning a higher income, leading organizations, and traveling more than in previous generations. Some of this ascension is hindered by the role of the national and family culture, which has prescribed and assigned roles of women in the society.

Challenges such as financial empowerment, views by men and the older generation, competition for promotion in the organization, ascribed and prescribed roles of women in Nigeria, societal norms, and family values are some of the issues Generation X women in positions of power face. Many women in the Generation X group are fast breaking away from these filial and society norms, and most do not consider the use of their cultural values while leading their organizations.

Three themes emerged from the study based on the three research questions: (a) There are clear differences and perspectives on the opinions of Generation X women in positions of power compared to those in the baby boomer generation. (b) Leadership of Generation X women in Nigeria is seen as an emerging trend. While many in the Generation X group respect culture and understand their roles in the family and society, their thinking is influenced by knowledge of worldviews, pop culture and the fast-paced flat, business environment. Many participants believed that with better knowledge of globalization issues and how they affect young generations, Generation X women in positions of power can use the opportunity of higher or advanced education as a tool for fighting oppression and achieve equality. This further knowledge and education can be viewed as a correlation to their selected leadership style. The more knowledge and education, the better a Generation X woman can be assertive in her opinions to speak her mind. (c) The leadership style characteristics of Generation X women are used as tools of empowerment and not as an ascribed or prescribed role of women in the society. They believed that the rules or organizational culture come first which assisted them in determining their leadership styles.

Three leadership styles, the democratic, situational, and transformational were utilized most often by the various participants in their day to day activities. One respondent selected the bureaucratic style because of her professional sector. None of the research participants selected the autocratic or laissez-faire styles of leadership. Those in management positions between the ages of 35-39 mostly selected the situational style. The younger participants ranging in ages of 30 to 34 selected the democratic style. Many of the participants from the South-West selected the democratic style of leadership as depicted in Figure 16. The younger the participants, the more they liked the democratic style of leadership and the ability to work in different teams. Several of the participants who were over the age of 40 selected the transformational style and felt the need to inspire and motivate employees. Many in this age group also had a little bit more life experience than the younger age groups.

Although all participants were of the Christian faith, and most were from the South, East, West, and Middle–Belt regions, some of the research participants worked in the Northern part of the country. The participants who worked in the Northern–Muslim part of Nigeria selected the situational style of leadership based on the educational level, religious beliefs, moral values and cultural norms of the Northern–Muslim part of the country. Several women of the Generation X group in Nigeria do not believe that they would like to change to a universal style of leadership even if it means leading effectively in the 21st century. They are proud of their culture and heritage and believe that western pop-culture is fast spreading across the globe.

Several Generation X Nigerian women in positions of power are judged and pressured to accept western leadership practices, depending on the sector in which they work. Most are happy to accept emerging trends and views of organizational leadership to make their work run smoother and to lead organizations effectively. Many, on the other hand believed that the job sector, type of team or staff they led and the organizational culture depicted their leadership styles.

SUMMARY

The objective of *Generation X: The Role of Culture on the Leadership Styles of Women in Leadership Positions* was to investigate the leadership styles of Nigerian women belonging to the Generation X sub-culture. The study and actual research phases involved the participation of 50 women leaders from Nigeria. An open-ended survey questionnaire was disseminated to understand participants' perspectives and interpret perceptions of the role of culture on leadership characteristics, drawn from the lived experiences of Generation X women leaders in Nigeria. The Van Kaam (1994) method of data presentation for determining themes and patterns was used in the study to understand the day–to–day leadership experiences of Generation X women in positions of power in Nigeria.

This method was also used to understand the perception of Generation X women, and how they view and use the power within the organization based on the present societal and environmental mores present in the Nigerian society. A phenomenological study gathered insights and explored the personal experiences of women leaders in Nigeria, to provide a deeper understanding of how Nigerian women leaders perceive the influence of contradictory cultural influences on their views, the use of power within the organization, and on their leadership styles (Okpara, 2007).

Background of Research

Organizational power and politics permeate all actions within an organization. Power is one person's ability to exert change on another person's way of life and actions (Sweeney & McFarlin, 2002). Using power is a valuable means of influencing and achieving intended desires and future action in others. Power is instrumental; it is a means of achieving goals other than the attainment of power itself.

The works of Karl Marx in the 19th century and Max Weber in the 20th century showed that Elitist theories, such as social class and economic structure, sometimes determine the ways in which leaders use power (Christian & Howson, 2009). According to pluralist theories, a group member's success is dependent on the appropriateness of the particular power tactics, leadership styles, and political dynamics he or she employs with others in the group (Christian, 2008). Marxist's theories of power state that a person can hold power as a result of economic and political influence in the society; not necessarily because the person holds an elected office or holds positions of power within an organization (Christian & Howson, 2009).

Hofstede (1980, 1991, 1994, 2001) developed a cultural dimension model based on a research study done in 67 countries. In the study, he discussed the influence of culture on individual behavior. Hofstede identified four dimensions:

Power distance: This cultural element describes the degree of inequality among people who are considered acceptable.

Individualism/collectivism: This element implies a loosely knit social framework in which people take care of themselves and their immediate families only, whereas collectivism is characterized as a tight social framework in which people distinguish between in-groups and out-groups.

Masculinity/femininity: This element describes the degree to which values and traits in society are associated with masculine qualities.

Uncertainty avoidance: This element describes the extent to which a society can deal with threatening, ambiguous, or anxiety-provoking situations.

Long-term/short-term orientation: This element describes the degree to which members of the culture accept delayed rewards and gratification.

Overview of the Problem Statement

Women and leadership in Nigeria are an important social concern (Nwosu, 2006). Women in 21st century Nigeria have contributed notably to various organizations and have ascended to top leadership positions in their respective businesses and professions. Despite this escalation in rank, many women in positions of power face enormous problems in their abilities to lead organizations effectively based on societal values, norms, and beliefs. The workforce in Nigeria now includes a younger generation of women called Generation X. This generation is moving upward faster than their predecessors of women leaders based on the global business landscape.

The "universal" 21st century global market leadership culture is mostly guided by western ideologies that are in direct conflict with the national and family culture of Nigeria (Ahiauzu, 1984, Ejiofor, 1987, & Okpara, 1996). The Generation X women in positions of power seem to be caught between the Nigerian societal culture and that of the western business ideology of the 21st century. A societal culture that has prescribed and assigned roles for women, especially young women, often limits the potential of women leaders in the society and their power when they are in leadership positions. Other sources that limit the power of women are income, social class, political influence, and property. These influences can determine a person's ability to hold a position of power in the society (Thio, 1992).

Overview of the Research Questions

Research questions were developed through certain avenues that reconstructed a particular situation to focus exclusively on the experience of participants (Creswell, 2002). When studying the leadership styles of Generation X Nigerian women in positions of power in 21st century Nigerian organizations, several questions guided the research. The research questions were based on the problem statement.

The research questions for this study are as follows:

1. What are the general attitudes of peers and subordinates toward Generation X women in positions of power?

2. What role does societal culture play on the leadership styles of Generation X women?

3. How do Generation X women in positions of power view and use power within the organization?

The open-ended survey questionnaire circulated to Generation X Nigerian women in positions of power in select organizations showed the presence of young emerging Generation X women in leadership positions.

Emergent Themes

From the study outcome, three general themes emerged based on the research questions. The three emerging themes used for this study are as follows: (a) There are clear differences in opinions and perspectives of Generation X women in leadership positions compared to those of previous generations and men. (b) Leadership of Generation X women in Nigeria is still an emerging trend. (c) There are differences in the leadership styles or characteristics of Generation X women from the previous generation.

Primary Research Question One: *What are the general attitudes of peers and subordinates, including men towards Generation X women in positions of power?*

The intent of this question was to understand the treatment by peers and subordinates in the organizational environment, and how those in the immediate organizational environment view and treat young women leaders in Nigeria who exhibit different or certain leadership styles. From the findings, the data revealed that the perceptions of others, including peers, subordinates, men, and others within the organization, view Generation X women in a position of power with mixed reactions.

Some of these views are positive while others are negative. Some of the positive perceptions, as shown in Figure 4, depict that Generation X women in leadership positions are confident, professional, loyal to their peers and subordinates, and committed to the goals of the organization. On the mixed or negative side, the data findings showed that Generation X women are viewed with distrust, due to their young age, and treated as if they are incapable of leading an organization or managing people. Sometimes, they are viewed as stubborn, because they are too independent and have more choices than previous generations of women leaders.

Theme One: *There are clear differences in perspectives and opinions from the previous generation of women leaders in Nigeria, including men, on the leadership styles of Generation X women.*

The general theme from this question was that there were clear differences and perspectives on Generation X women in positions of power compared to those in the baby boomer generation, or men. These differing views all depend on the person's age, their level of education, years of experience, professional sector, exposure to others in a diverse and multi-cultural environment.

The ways in which Generation X women in positions of power were viewed were different from men, who see control or power as a natural phenomenon of their culture. Generation X women have to think of their femininity sometimes before they exercise their power when subordinates include older women and men in general. Furthermore, many Generation X women in positions of power have to think twice of what others think of them when they are around men and exercise leadership styles similar to those men use. This view cuts across borders in developing countries, where the role of culture is very prevalent in how women occupying positions often occupied by males are thought to behave, manage people or lead organizations.

Primary Research Question Two: *What role does societal culture play on the leadership styles of Generation X women in Nigeria?*

This question was asked to understand the day-to-day lived experiences from participants' views. These day-to-day lived experiences included challenges, obstacles, and positive and negative outcomes of how their leadership styles were influenced or not by their cultural beliefs, societal norms, religious practices, and family values. This question also sought to understand the role of how societal values expect Generation X women in positions of power to behave regardless of their positions of power.

From the findings, the data reflected were similar to the findings of the data on research question one. Depending on the age, level of education, professional sector, or cultural background, the findings of the data were that some of the participants' leadership styles were affected by cultural and environment mores present in the society. Other findings from the data already presented showed that culture did not affect the leadership styles of Generation X women in Nigeria.

This premise is based on the fact that Generation X women are seen by many as more exposed, more aware due to the global business environment, and more traveled; and they are able to mix with others easily and seek professional or business opportunities in areas where their leadership styles are based on the organizational culture and not on family or societal cultures. The findings of the data also reflected that some of the Generation X women in leadership positions kept their cultural and family values at the back of their minds and depending on the age of their subordinates, they exercised their cultural values on their leadership styles.

For example, many Nigerian family and societal norms give respect to men and those who are older despite the position a person occupies. Thus, findings from this data reflected that many of the participants were cognizant of the Nigerian national culture, in addition to their individual family cultures, which were based on the respect of others who were not only elderly but who, in general, were also from different regions due to the different cultural values present in Nigeria. For example, two of the participants who worked in the Northern part of the country stated that they did let their cultural values influence their leadership styles because of the Northern–Muslim traditions. Hence, these two participants selected the situation leadership style, based on the people they led and the environment in which they were based. Their culture did influence their leadership styles.

Theme Two: *Leadership of Generation X women in Nigeria is an emerging trend.*

The general theme from this question was that leadership of Generation X women in Nigeria is seen as an emerging trend. While many in the Generation X group respect the culture and understand their roles in the family and society, their thinking is influenced by knowledge of worldviews, pop culture and the fast-paced, flat business environment. Many believe that with better knowledge, women can use education as a tool in fighting oppression and as a correlation to their leadership styles. The more knowledge and education, the better a Generation X woman can be assertive in her opinions and speak her mind.

The findings from the data for this theme reflected that Nigeria, like many countries, is still behind in having women advancing into leadership positions. In this regard, views of participants, based on the findings of the data were that women who are known in Nigeria in leadership positions are those in the baby boomer generations who fought in post–colonial independent Nigeria and are still fighting to have more qualified women in positions of power. The new generation of emerging women leaders of the Generation X group are ascending faster in leadership positions than their counterparts, the baby boomers. Generation X women attained higher levels of education and are more financially independent than baby boomers. Therefore, they have better choices in terms of career and family.

Generation X women in positions of power are ascending faster than their counterparts, the baby boomers, in professional and business sectors due to the availability of better and informed choices. Findings from the study showed that the news of the leadership of Generation X women in positions of power and the rate in which they are ascending to leadership positions in Nigeria.

Previous generations, such as baby boomers, are still fighting for equality and struggling in their leadership positions to maintain gender parity in certain key positions within certain businesses and organizations in Nigeria. Data from the findings reflected that several of the participants had family values which did not respect young women in leadership positions, despite the regions they were from in Nigeria or their ethnic groups. News of Generation X women in positions of power is an emerging trend which many, including males, previous generations of women leaders, and subordinates with diverse and multi-cultural perspectives are growing to accept in the Nigerian socio–economic and national culture.

Findings from data collected reflected that Nigerians, while still getting used to baby boomers attaining high leadership positions in the country, are also just getting used to having younger women in positions of power. The general idea from the findings of this theme was that women's leadership in general is an emerging trend in Nigeria, whether the women were from the baby boomer generation or from the Generation X group. For the Generation X women in positions of power, their young age, fast ascension to leadership positions and educational or knowledge attainment are sometimes considered as a threat to both men and the baby boomer generation of women leaders. In general, Generation X women in positions of power in Nigeria are encouraged by the baby boomer generation in the society and other women who want the best for females advancing in Nigeria. These previous generations of women in the society encourage Generation X women in leadership positions due to their own struggles to break the glass ceilings. Other generations of women in Nigeria believe in the tradition and culture of the society, as in many Sub-Saharan African countries, where it is the belief that women need to take charge of their familial duties based on societal and cultural expectations.

Primary Research Question Three: *How do Generation X women in positions of power in Nigeria view and use power within the organization?*

The intent of this question was to understand from participants' perspectives what they believed they could accomplish in the organization with their statuses in leadership positions. This question also sought to understand the view and perspectives of Generation X women in positions of power in Nigeria and how they relate their leadership styles to their environment. Findings from the data of this theme reflected that Generation X women in positions of power view their leadership positions as an opportunity amidst the national and family culture prevalent in the Nigerian society.

This opportunity, the data showed, is based on the fact that Generation X women have more advantages and are more knowledgeable due to the economic and global business landscape. They also view power as the ability to have others to complete the tasks to achieve the organizational goals. The findings from the data showed that Generation X women in positions of power like team environment approaches to their leadership within their organizations and businesses. On the answer to the research question, many of the participants selected the democratic leadership style, where everyone has something to contribute to the goals of the organization and not one where they have to dictate in an authoritarian or bureaucratic nature.

Theme Three: *Differences in leadership styles of Generation X women*

The general theme from this research question was that the leadership style characteristics of Generation X women are used as tools of empowerment and not as an ascribed or prescribed role of women in the society. They believe that the rules or organizational culture comes first, which assists them in determining their leadership styles. From the findings of the data, the leadership styles of Generation X women in Nigeria are mostly based on the professional sector and the organizational culture where they exercise their leadership styles.

Hofstede (1980) defined culture as the collective programming of the mind that distinguishes the members of a group from another. Hofstede (1980, 1991, 1994, and 2001) developed a cultural dimension model based on a research study done in 67 countries. In the study, he discussed the influence of culture on individual behavior. Hofstede identified five dimensions: (a) Power distance, (b) Individualism/collectivism, (c) Masculinity/femininity, (d) Uncertainty avoidance, (e) Long-term/short-term orientation.

Hostede's five dimensions of power can be applied to the third theme and to the overall study in general, because Generation X women in positions of power sometimes exercise their leadership styles based on the cultural influence on a leader's individual behavior. Many of the participants of the study occasionally based their leadership styles on the power distance between their selected leadership styles and their current environment, including the organizational culture. Participants viewed power from an individual basis of the set goals and targets that needed to be achieved in the organization and stakeholder demands.

Sometimes, they viewed power from a collective approach, or that of a democratic or transformational leadership style, where they gave subordinates the opportunity to provide input to team projects and lead by example. Generation X women in positions of power who participated in the study used power for both long and short-term orientation, such as when goals and tasks were to be met. They also used power to related to their peers and subordinates and view others based on how subordinates related to the Generation X woman leader in a team environment with an uncertainty avoidance situation.

Limitations

The study was limited to women in positions of power who were between the ages of 30 to 45 years of age. This research was also limited to a few participants, numbering in 30 people, a fact which did not reflect the views of all Generation X women in leadership positions in the whole of Nigeria. The participants in the study were all of the Christian faith and the majority of them were from the South. The researcher sought participants from diverse backgrounds to include variety in the following categories: culture, religion, economics, education, and management experience. Due to time constraints, only a select number of people were willing to participate in the research. The general purpose of this research was to gather the day-to-day leadership experiences of Generation X women in positions of power in Nigeria. This goal of the study was met despite the limitation of other ethnic, religious, and social backgrounds of people present in Nigeria.

Significance to Leadership

This study explored the day-to-day leadership styles of Generation X women in positions of power in Nigeria and how culture affects their leadership styles. The significance of this qualitative phenomenological study on the role of culture in the leadership styles of Generation X women in Nigeria was that there are differences in opinions from men, previous generations, such as baby boomers, and peers about Generation X women in leadership positions. The second core theme was that learning about leadership styles of a new generation of women leaders is an emerging trend. The third core theme was that Generation X women have differing views about their positions of power, depending on the professional sector and culture of the area of Nigeria that they work in.

The first core theme on the treatment of leadership of Generation X women by others was seen as differing based on several demographics of the men, the previous generation of women leaders, and subordinates. These demographic factors were level of education, family background, exposure to young women in their families attaining leadership positions, social backgrounds, the professional sector or business in which they worked, and whether there were young women in leadership positions there. Environmental awareness to women's issues, such as women's rights and equality campaigns in the national culture, also determined how others view or treat Generation X women in leadership positions.

Issues pertaining to women in the workforce attaining leadership positions in the 21st century should not be seen as the younger generation competing with the baby boomers, but as equality in the workforce, based on qualifications and knowledge of managing an organization in a 21st century global market. The issue of equality for women on the job is wide-spread across different countries, where women are fighting to attain higher levels of leadership positions and to have the opportunity to sit at their organizations' negotiating tables to prove themselves. Understanding issues, such as women trying to break the glass ceiling, younger women attaining higher levels of education in Nigeria, and more women being independent and having their own businesses or leading their own organizations, all assist in changing how others treat Generation X women in positions of power.

The significance of the second core theme to leadership as an emerging trend is that Nigerians, in general, are still getting used to having more women in positions of power in various sectors in the country and time is still needed to become fully aware of the potential and contributions of Generation X women in positions of power in Nigeria. The younger the generation of men and subordinates, the better the treatment of Generation X women in positions of power. The much older generation has a traditionalist view of the societal culture and norms and assigned roles of women in the society. The significance of the emerging leadership of Generation X women in Nigeria shows that Nigeria, especially younger generations, is welcoming more women leaders, and people have a more diversified worldview, and a better perspective on how women in general, and particularly those in the Generation X sub-group, can be as effective in leading or managing organizations amidst the prevalent national and societal cultures.

The significance of the third core theme is to demonstrate how Generation X women in positions of power view and use power within their organizations, and how their leadership styles vary, dependent on the organizations' cultures and the individuals they manage on a daily basis. Based on the study, many of the participants between 34-39 years of age selected the democratic style of leadership, because they liked to work with people in diverse environments and the opportunity to include everyone's input on projects or contribute to the organizations' goals. Others who selected the situational style of leadership explained that the opportunity to exert or exercise different leadership styles was based on professional sectors, regions, customer bases, and the day-to-day activities within the organizational environment, not external factors such as the societal and cultural values or norms. Data from the study also signified to leadership that the older the Generation X women in positions of power were, such as those over 40, the more they used the transformational leadership styles based on their professional and family experiences in the society.

Those between the ages of 40 to 45 who selected the transformational leadership style were closely related to the baby boomers and learned from that generation. For the baby boomer generation, their filial duties based on family and societal mores prevents them from being as independent as Generation X women, who can delay being in the family duty. Also, it was observed from the study that even when Generation X women wanted to break the glass ceiling, and even though they were bound by the family or national culture, they were more outgoing and could easily adapt to the organizational culture based on the already present multi-ethnic and diverse Nigerian society.

Thus, it can be assumed from the findings of the study that environmental adaptation to global and environmental trends assists Generation X women in positions of power to exercise various leadership styles that are not based on national or family culture, but on that of the organizational environment. This is coupled with the ease of Generation X women in positions of power to adapt to the current global business culture of working with diverse groups of people. Learning about and adapting new technologies to their everyday lives and their ability to make better independent choices are both different characteristcs that they posses from previous generations of women in similar positions.

Based on the three core themes that originated from the study, the results can assist in adjusting some of the cultural biases that women face on the job. This study can also assist organizational leaders to view Generation X women in positions of power as being capable of leading a 21st century organization due to their scope of knowledge about the flat and growing business landscape that many of them have blended into, due to new technologies and innovations in the business environment. In addition, this study can serve as a model for inter-cultural or multi-cultural business organizations, in which diverse people from different ethnic, educational, religious, social, and economic classes are capable of using their opportunities as women leaders to encourage and mentor other younger generations of women leaders to attain leadership positions.

SWOT ANALYSIS

For this study, this is the general SWOT analysis of the strengths, weaknesses, opportunities, and threats of the research findings and the significance to leadership. A SWOT analysis is a four-part approach that organizational leaders use in analyzing the overall strategy of an organization in relation to that of its competitors or external stakeholders. A SWOT analysis can be conducted to identify some of the factors that are affecting an organization's ability to be competitive in the global market. Conducting a SWOT analysis can assist the organization in understanding the direction in which the goal or the organization is heading (Collete, 1999 & Simmering, 2006). For this study, the following are the SWOT analyses as derived from the research findings.

Strengths

The Generation X women's ability to excel and advance in leadership positions at the same or a faster pace than their counterparts from different generations or genders is a common strength. There is a global trend where women in general, whether in developed or developing countries, are fighting a common struggle to attain higher levels of leadership positions. Generation X women, unlike their predecessors, the post-independence baby boomer generation, are more adaptable and can exercise different leadership styles without letting their filial duties or environmental mores affect their leadership or interaction with their subordinates, peers or men in general.

Weaknesses

The young age of Generation X women in positions of power, men in similar positions or men in general who are peers and subordinates, and older females in the same or similar positions, are some of the weaknesses of the significance to leadership of Generation X women in positions of power. Another weakness is the national and family culture in Nigeria in general. There are still some areas, sectors, business avenues, professional sectors and other areas in leadership in Nigeria where Generation X women in positions of power have not yet arrived. Some industries with important male presences, where men are known to be in leading roles and structures, are still off grounds to many Generation X women in positions of power. Such areas with limited women leadership include politics, the military, markets and financial institutions, and general social support structures.

Opportunities

More Generation X women are advancing faster in the 21st century than the women leaders from the post–independence generation of women leaders. Nigeria's economy is good and stable, which provides an opportunity for the advancement of Generation X women in Nigeria. A good economy yields positive business growth, a stable market, and better advancement of opportunities. The ability to capitalize on new products, information, business partnerships and services, and the ability to establish new business ventures, are opportunities for Generation X women in leadership positions to excel. Expanded business opportunities or growing markets will ensure opportunities with more women leaders in the business and professional environment in the future.

Access to new and improved technology and global trends will be a crucial educational force for Generation X women in leadership positions, because the future Generation Y will have better access and knowledge than Generation X or their predecessors, the baby boomers.

Future opportunities for Generation X women in positions of power include the business environment and sector in which Generation X women work, where their performance and ability to achieve set goals, produce results and meet targets can have more Generation X women in better leadership positions and help them become more financially capable of owning more production means.

Future opportunities, such as the capability of Generation X women to exercise their leadership styles and to meet the 21st century globalized market standards and the ability to be able to compete with their peers and subordinates, will have many more Generation X women promoted based on performance or economic stability in the country. New business sectors will have better opportunities and accept more women in leadership positions.

Threats

The global trends, where Generation X women have to compete with women in western countries for positions in certain sectors, sometimes with conflicting cultures, are a big threat to Generation X women in positions of power. Men of any age and in any position are a threat to Generation X women in positions of power due to cultural factors and the ways in which some females are expected to behave around men in the society. Certain positions considered to be "macho" or male oriented are threats to Generation X women in leadership positions. Older women with similar or more experience are a threat to Generation X women in positions of power because Generation X women have to double proof themselves and their skills and sometimes compete with women whom in the society they may consider as their elders. Another threat to Generation X women in leadership positions is that their subordinates may not respect their leadership positions because of their age.

Future threats for Generation X women in positions of power are the next Generation–Generation Y—who will be the emerging trend for Generation X. The Generation Y members are more technologically savvy than many Generation X members, and they base their awareness and knowledge on the availability of new technology. Many in Generation X can adapt easily to organizational and environmental threats, but may find it more competitive in keeping up with the next generation after them, the Generation Y group and newer technologies. In general, Generation X will lead their teams based on awareness of global trends and their adaptability to current, available technology in the business environment if the threat from men and the baby boomer generation is too much.

Implications for Future Research

The current study focused on the Generation X women sub–group in positions of power in Nigeria. This research was conducted to validate the research questions and the questionnaire that was administered to research participants as a base for further studies that can be developed from some of their responses as specified by the research participants. The implication of the findings of research for future study is that a more in-depth study could be conducted on both the Generation X and baby boomer groups for a comparative analysis on the three emerging themes and the views of baby boomers directly on the leadership styles of Generation X women in Nigeria. Applying a different research methodology, such as an ethnographic study, for an in-depth social impact study could be conducted with new information that was not included in the original research due to limitations from previous studies. A different pool of study participants based on a new set of demographics could be studied for new emerging themes based on current and future environmental and societal factors present in Nigeria.

The implications of the results of the current study can also be used for future research on the region, industry, and the other demographic factors that were generated from the current participant's answers to understand the day-to-day leadership experiences of Generation X group from a specific region in Nigeria compared to another region. For example, the study could yield results or new data about why many of the participants who worked in or hailed from the Southern part of Nigeria selected the democratic style of leadership as compared to those who worked in the North and selected the situational style of leadership.

Recommendations

The analyzed results from the data of this research can be used by organizational leaders in Nigeria to understand leadership of young women as an emerging trend and issues—such as striving to break the glass ceiling, gender equality issues across the globe, better access to finances and financial institutions, and better opportunities to social support structures—can both assist organizational leaders to understand some of the biases toward women and leadership in Nigeria.

Organizational leaders, who conduct business internationally or in cross-cultural environments, can understand the lived-experiences of Generation X women in positions of power in Nigeria so that they do not fail in efforts to improve organizational goals and strategies. The goals and strategies of organizations improve in instances where the workforce is diversified to include a younger generation of leaders, such as women and those from various multi-cultural backgrounds in leadership and management positions. Organizational goals and strategies also improve when business leaders understand how Generation X women working in a multi-cultural environment view and use power in day-to-day leadership positions (Chan & Mauborgne, 2009).

The significance of the study to the general body of Nigerian women leaders and their various leadership styles strengthens their influence, which may serve to the building of highly effective and functioning teams, to increase team performance, improve competitiveness, innovation, and creativity of team members. The study could be extended to further assist women organizational leaders as a recommendation or blueprint for growth in leadership styles. This study provided preliminary research into how the national culture of Nigeria affects Generation X women leaders in 21st century organizations in Nigeria. In the future, this research may model good leadership styles and workforce diversity for the younger generations of women leaders in positions of power, whether they work Nigeria or in any multi-national company or international organization.

CONCLUSION

The research in this book provided insight into the background of the study, including the problem statement, the significance, the nature of the study, and the research questions. A presentation of the phenomenological qualitative methodology was based on a study conducted by Hofstede's (1980, 1991, 1994, 2001) cultural-dimension model where he identified five relationships that appeared useful in describing the relationship of culture to management and leadership, in addition to Bass (1990) transformational leadership theory.

The data analysis of the research findings were presented using the Van Kaam (1994) methods and Creswell (2005) steps. The research was triangulated when the researcher confirmed from the respondents the questionnaire answers that completed the research for validity and reliability. It was determined that data saturation was established after several of the survey questionnaires produced the same patterns and themes needed for the study.

The overview of the background of the study, the problem statement, research questions, the emergent themes, significance to leadership, the implication for further research, the summary and conclusions were also presented. Three themes emerged from the study based on the three research questions: (a) Leadership of Generation X women in Nigeria is seen as an emerging trend. While many in the Generation X group respect the culture and understand their roles in the family and society, their thinking is influenced by knowledge of worldviews, pop culture, and the fast-paced, flat business environment. Many believe that with better knowledge, women can use education as a tool in fighting oppression and as a correlation to their leadership styles. The more knowledge and education, the better a Generation X woman can be assertive in the opinions to speak her mind. (b) There are clear differences and perspectives in the opinions of Generation X women in positions of power, compared to those in the baby boomer generation. (c) The leadership style characteristics of Generation X women are used as tools of empowerment and not as ascribed or prescribed roles of women in the society. Participants of the study believed that the rules or organizational culture came first, a fact which assisted them in determining their leadership styles.

The role of culture on the leadership styles of Generation X women in Nigeria is seen as an emerging trend, where younger generations of women are ascending the professional ladder faster. More women are earning higher incomes, leading organizations, and traveling more than in previous generations. Some of this ascension is hindered by the role of the national and family culture that has prescribed and assigned the role of women in the society.

Challenges such as financial empowerment, views by men and the older generations, competition for promotion in the organization, ascribed and prescribed roles of women in Nigeria, societal norms, and family values are some of the obstacles Generation X women in positions of power face. Many women in the Generation X group are quickly breaking away from these filial and societal norms, and most do not consider the use of their cultural values while leading their organizations.

The topic of women and leadership is a cross-cutting issue across the globe, and it does not only include Nigeria but many countries. The Generation X group is a fast-growing trend in organizational leadership, and the same issues that apply to Generation X women in Nigeria may apply to women in other countries, especially in Sub-Saharan Africa where culture significantly affects women in positions of power. According to Bing (2004), Hofstede's work provided practical applications in cross-cultural training and development to help people work more effectively in more than one culture.

Application of the dimensions of cross-cultural leadership can help people understand their cultural tendencies. Regarding the different models of leadership presented in this book, people need to understand that leadership practices and expectations may differ internationally, regionally, and even nationally. Further recommendations for this study are that organizational leaders can use it to understand the leadership styles of Generation X women in Nigeria and why they apply different aspects of French and Raven's (1960) five identified sources of power which coercive, reward, legitimate, expert, and referent—in leading their organizations and in managing the people that they lead.

Generation X women in positions of power can adapt to any other generation, peer, or subordinate, both women and men. Generation X women in positions of power can adapt their leadership styles to the national and family cultures that are present in Nigeria. They are also more adaptable to current, new, and improved technologies than any other generation. Generation X women in positions of power, therefore, can be compared to the chameleon, which is adaptable in any situation.

REFERENCES

Ahuja, M. K. (2002). Women in the information technology profes sion: A literature review, synthesis, and research agenda. *European Journal of Information Systems*, 11. 20–34.

Alapo, R. (2013). The Role of Culture on the Leadership Styles of Women in Nigeria: A Phenomenological Study. *University of Phoenix, School of Advanced Studies Publishing*.

Atwater, L., Avolio, B. J., & Bass, B. M. (1996). The transformational and transactional leadership of men and women. *International Review of Applied Psychology*, 45. 5-34.

Avolio, B. J., Bhatia, P., Koh, W., & Zhu, W. (2004). Transformational leadership and organizational commitment: Mediating role of psychological empowerment and moderating role of structural distance. *Journal of Organizational Behavior*, 25. 951-968.

Avolio, B. J., & Bass, B. M. (1995). Transformational leadership and organizational culture. *Public Administration Quarterly*, 17. 112-122.

Bass, B.M. (1999). Two decades of research and development in transformational leadership. *European Journal of Work and Organizational Psychology*, 8(1). 9-32.

Bass, B.M. 1997. Does the transactional–transformational leadership paradigm transcend organizational and national boundaries? *American Psychologist* 52(2). 130-139.

Bass, B. M., & Avolio, B. J. (1994). Improving organizational effectiveness through transformational leadership. Thousand Oaks, CA: Sage.

Bass, B. M. (1990). *Bass and Stogdill's handbook of leadership: Theory, research, & managerial applications* (3rd. ed.). New York: The Free Press.

Bass, B. (Win, 1990). From transactional to transformational leadership: learning to share the vision. *Organizational Dynamics*, 18(3). 19-31.

Bass, B. (1989). *Stogdill's Handbook of Leadership: A Survey of Theory and Research*. New York: Free Press.

Bass, B. M. (1985). *Leadership and performance beyond expectations*. Free Press, New York, NY.

Bernardi, J., & Mahedi, W. (1994). *A generation alone: Xers making a place in the world. St. Louis*, IL: Intervarsity Press.

Bolman, L. G. and Deal, T. E. (2003). *Reframing organizations: art istry, choice, and leadership* (3rd ed.). San Francisco: Jossey-Bass.

Bradberry, T., Eberlin, R., Kottraba, C., & Tatum, B.C. (2005). Leadership, decision-making, and organizational justice. *Management Decision*, 41. 1006-1016.

Bryman, A. (1987). The generalization of implicit leadership theory. *Journal of Social Psychology*, 127(2). 129-141.

Burns, J.M. (1978). *Leadership*. New York: Harper & Row.

Brownlee, J., Nailon, D., & Tickle, E. L. (2005). Personal epistemological beliefs and transformational leadership behaviours. *Journal of Management Development*, 24. 706-719.

Brinkley, D. (1994). Educating the generation called X: Stop making sense of Generation X. *Washington Post Education Review*.1.

Celek, T., & Zander, D. (1996). *Inside the soul of a new generation*. Grand Rapid, MI: Zondervan.

Christian, M. (2009). Assessing class: wealth. *Stratification and class in the US. EBSCO research starters*.

Cherniss, C. & Goleman, D. (Eds.). (2001). *The emotionally intelligent workplace*. San Francisco: Jossey-Bass.

Choi, J.N. (2004). Individual and contextual dynamics of innovation-use behavior in organizations. *Human Performance*, 17(4). 397-414.

Cooper, D. R., & Schindler, P. S. (2003). *Business research methods* (8th ed.). New York: McGraw-Hill Higher Education.

Coupland, D. (2000). *Generation X: Tales for an accelerated culture*. New York, NY: St. HarperCollins Publishers.

Darity, W.A, Jr. (2008). *Leadership. International Encyclopedia of the Social Sciences*. Ed. (4), 2nd ed. Detroit: Macmillan Reference USA.

Dastmalchian, A., Javidan, M. & Alam, K. (2001). 'Effective leadership and culture in Iran: An empirical study'. *Applied*

Psychology: An International Review, 50(4). 532-558.

Dembner, A. (1998). Poll finds college students ready to make a difference back on campus. *Boston Globe*, 9. 1.

Dorfman, P. (1996). International and cross-cultural leadership, In: Punnett, B.J., and Shenkar, O., eds., *Handbook for International Management Research*. MA: Blackwell Publisher. 267-349.

Dubois, E. C. (2006). Three decades of women's history. *Women's Studies*, 35(1). 47-64.

Dunne, M. (1997). Policy leadership, Generation X style. *National Civic Review*, 86(3). 10-17.

Drucker, P. (2002, August). The Discipline of Innovation. Entrepreneuriship. *Harvard Business Review*.

Eagly, A. H. and Johnson, B. T. (1990). Gender and leadership style: A meta-analysis. *Psychological Bulletin*, 108(2). 233-257.

Ejiofor, P.N.O. 1987. *Management in Nigeria: Theories and Issues. Onitsha*. Nigeria: Longman.

Evans, M. G. (1996). R. J. House's a path-goal theory of leader effectiveness. *Leadership Quarterly*, 3. 305-310.

Frize, M. (2005). Proceedings of the 2005 *ACM International Conference on Women in Leadership: Value of women's contributions in science, engineering, and technology*. Baltimore, MD.

Fuchs, C., & Hofkirchner, W. (2005). Self-organization, knowledge, and responsibility. Kybernetes, 34(1/2). 241-260.

Gallivan, M. J. (2004). Examining IT professionals' adaptation to technological change: The influence of gender and personal attributes. Advances in Information Systems, 35(3). 28-49.

Gazso, A. (2004). Women's inequality in the workplace as framed in news discourse: Refracting from gender ideology. T*he Canadian Review of Sociology and Anthropology*. 41. 449-473.

Georges, C. (1994, Jan 31). The boring twenties: Grow up, crybabies, you're America's luckiest generation. *The Washington Post*. 27.

Gibson, C. B. (1995). An investigation of gender differences in leadership across four Countries. *Journal of International Busi-*

ness Studies. 26(2). 255 -280.

Gordon, R., & Grant, D. (2005). Knowledge management or management of knowledge? why people interested in knowledge management need to consider foucault and the construct of power. *TAMARA Journal of Critical Postmodern Organization Science*, 3(2).27–38.

Hanges, P. J., Lord, R. G.,Dickson, M. W., (2000). An information-processing perspective on leadership and culture: A case for Connectionist architecture. *Applied Psychology-An International Review*, 49(1). 133-161.

Hautala, T. (2005). The effects of subordinates' personality on appraisals of transformational leadership. *Journal of Leadership & Organizational Studies*, 11(4). 84-93.

Helland, M. R., & Winston, B. E. (2005). Towards a deeper understanding of hope and leadership. *Journal of Leadership & Organizational Studies*, 12(2). 42-55.

Hofstede, G. (2001). *Culture's consequences: Comparing values, behaviors, institutions and organizations across nations.* Thousand Oaks, CA: Sage.

Hofstede, G. (1994). Business cultures. *UNESCO Courier*, 4. 12-16.

Hofstede, G. (1993). Cultural constraints in management theories. *Academy of Management Executives*, 7. 81-94.

Hofstede, G., Bond, M. H., & Luk, C. L. (1993). Individual perceptions of organizational cultures: A methodological treaties on levels of analysis. *Organizational Studies.* 14. 483-503.

Hofstede, G. (1991). *Culture and organizations.* New York: Harper Collins.

Hofstede, G., & Bond, M. H. (1988). The Confucius connection: From cultural roots to economic growth. *Organization Dynamics*, 16(4). 4-21.

Hofstede, G. (1987). The applicability of McGregor's theories in south-east Asia. *Journal of Management Development*, 6(3). 9-18.

Hofstede, G. (1980). *Culture's consequence: International differences in workrelated values.* Beverly Hills, CA: Sage.

Holmberg, I & Åkerblom, S. (2006). Modelling leadership—implicit leadership theories in Sweden. *Scandinavian Journal of Management*, 22(4). 307-329.

House, R. J. et al. (2004). *Culture, leadership, and organizations: The GLOBE study of 62 societies.* Sage Publications.

Howe, N., & Strauss, W. (1992b). *Generations: The history of America's future, 1584 to 2069.* New York, NY: William Morrow and Company.

Hunt, G. I., Osborn, N. R., & Shermerhorn, R., Jr. (1991). *Organizational behavior.* New York: John Wiley & Sons.

Jogulu, U. D., & Wood, G. J. (2006). The role of leadership theory in raising the profile of women in management. *Equal Opportunities International*, 25(4). 236-250.

Jung, D.I., Bass, B.M., and Sosik, J.J. (1995). Bridging leadership and culture: A theoretical consideration of transformational leadership and collectivistic cultures. *The Journal of Leadership Studies*, 2(4). 3-18.

Keller, T. (2003). Parental images as a guide to leadership sense making: an attachment perspective on implicit leadership theory. *The Leadership Quarterly*, 14. 141-160.

Kedia, B. L., Nordtvedt, R., & Perez, L. M. (2002). International business strategies, decision-making theories, and leadership styles: An integrated framework. *Competitiveness Review,* 12(1). 38-52.

Kennerly, S. M., & McGuire, E. (2006). Nurse managers as transformational and transactional leaders. *Nursing Economics*, 24(4). 179-186.

Kleiner, A., and Sable, D. (2007). Organizational Change. *Encyclopedia of Business,* 2nd Ed.

Kriger, M & Seng, Y. (2005). Leadership with inner meaning: A contingency theory of leadership based on the worldviews of five religions. *Leadership Quarterly*, 16. 771-806.

Ladd, E. C. (1994). The twenty somethings: Generation myths' revisited. *The Public Perspective.* January/February. 14-18.

Lee, W. L. (2001). Leadership. *Encyclopedia of Business and Finance.* (2). New York: Macmillan Reference USA.

Lemons, M. A., & Parzinger, R. L. (2007). Gender schemas: A cognitive explanation of discrimination of women in technology. *Journal of Business and Psychology*, 22(1). 91–99.

Levy, F. (1999). *Dollars and dreams*. London, England: Sage.

Manning, T. T. (2004). Gender, managerial level, transformational leadership, and work satisfaction. *Women in Management Review*, 17(5/6), 207-216.

Madzar, S. (2005). Subordinates' information inquiry in uncertain times: a cross-cultural consideration of leadership style effect. *International Journal of Cross-Cultural Management*, 5(3). 255-273.

Markus, HR & Kitayama, S. (1991). Culture and the self: Implications for cognition, emotion, and Motivation. *Psychological Review*, 98. 224-253.

Matveev, A. and Lvina, L. (2007, July). *Effective transformational leadership across cultures: The role of cross-cultural communication competencies. WCA: Communication in the 21st Century: Exploring Roots; Expanding Visions*. Paper presented at the WCA Conference, Brisbane, Australia.

Mastenbroek, W.F.G. (Jan 2005). Emotion management, status competition, and power play. Organizational behavior in historical perspective.

McCabe, R., & Naude, M. (2005). Increasing retention: Aspects of management and leadership. *Australian Bulletin of Labour*, 31. 426-439.

McShane, S. and Travagelione. (2003). *Power, politics, and persuasion: Organizational behavior on the Pacific Rim*. McGraw-Hill Australia.

Michael, J. (1997). A conceptual framework for aligning managerial behaviors with cultural work values. *International Journal of Commerce and Management*, 7(3/4). 81-101.

Morrissey, C. S., & Schmidt, M. L. (2008, October). Fixing the system, not the women: An innovative approach to faculty advancement. *Journal of Women's Health*, 17(8). 1399.

Muenjohn, N. & Armstrong, A. (2007). Transformational leader ship: The influence of culture on the leadership behaviours of expatriate managers. *International Journal of Business and*

Information, 2(2). 265-283.

Muller, R., & Turner, R. (2005). The project manager's leadership style as a success factor on projects: A literature review. *Project Management Journal*, 36(1). 49-61.

Noll, C.L. (2001). Management: Authority and responsibility. *Encyclopedia of Business and Finance*. (2). New York: Macmillan.

Nwosu, B.U. (Dec. 2006). Civil society and electoral mandate protection in south-eastern Nigeria. *International Journal of Not-for-profit Law*, 9(1). 20.

Okpara, J.,O. (2007). The effect of culture on job satisfaction and organizational commitment: A study of information system managers in Nigeria. *Journal of African Business*, 8(1). 113-130.

Okpara, J. (1996). "An examination of the relationship of motivation needs, cultural factors, and job satisfaction among managers in selected business enterprises in Nigeria." Unpublished doctoral dissertation, New York University, New York.

Osiruemu, E. (2004). Women in the Trade Union Movement in Nigeria: The Constraints. *JENDA: A Journal of Culture and African Women Studies*. 6.

Palumbo, D.J. (1969, May – June). Power and role specificity in organization theory. *Public Administration Review*,29(3. 237-248.

Paulin, G., & Riordon, B. (1998). Making it on their own: The baby boomer meets Generation X. *Monthly Labor Review*, 121(2). 10-22.

Rausch, E. (2005). Guidelines for management and leadership decision. *Management Decision*. 4(10), 79-88.

Rodriguez, C. (1996). *International management: A cultural approach*. Mason, OH: South-Western.

Rojas, M. (1994). Women in pre-colonial a. African post-colonial literature in English in post – colonial web.

Rosner, J. B. (1990, Nov – Dec.) Ways women lead. *Harvard Business Review*. 119-125.

Russell, R. F., & Tucker, B. A. (2004). The influence of the transformational leader. *Journal of Leadership & Organizational*

Studies, 10(4). 103-112.

Strauss, W., & Howe, N. (1991). *Generations: The history of America's future, 1584 to 2069.* New York, NY: William Morrow & Company.

Spreitzer, G.M.; Perttula, K.H.; and Xin, K. (2005). Traditionality matters: an examination of the effectiveness of transformational leadership in the United States and Taiwan. *Journal of Organizational Behavior*, 26. 205-227.

Sashkin, M. (1988). *The visionary leader, in: Conger, J. A.; Kanungo, R. A. eds.: Charismatic Leadership: The elusive factor in organizational effectiveness.* San Francisco, Jossey-Bass.

Scott, R. W. (2003). *Organizations: Rational, natural, and open systems.* Upper Saddle River, NJ: Prentice Hall.

Soonhee, K. (2005). Factors affecting state government information technology employee turnover intentions. *American Review of Public Administration*, 35(2). 137-156.

Suk-Hing Chan, D. (2009). Relationship between generation-responsive leadership behaviors and job satisfaction of generation X and Y Professionals. Unpublished dissertation: University of Phoenix, Arizona.

Sweeney, P.D., and McFarlin, D.B. (2002). *Power and influence: Exercising leadership and practicing politics: Organizational behavior: solutions for management.* McGraw-Hill, Higher Education.

Thyer, G. (2004). Dare to be different: Transformational leadership may hold the key to reducing the nursing shortage. *Journal of Nursing Management*, 11. 73-79.

Tulgan, B. (2000). *Managing Generation X.* New York, NY: W.W. Norton & Company.

Torpman, J. (2004). The differentiating function of modern forms of leadership. *Management Decision*,42. 892-902.

Triandis, HC. (1989). The self and social behavior in differing cultural context. *Psychological Review*, 96(3). 506-520.

Victor, D.A., and Turner, M.C. (2006). Leadership styles and bases of power. *Encyclopedia of Management.* Ed. Marilyn M. Helms. 5th ed. Detroit: Gale. 442-445.

Webb, K. S. (Spr. 2009). Why emotional intelligence should matter to management: A survey of the literature. *SAM Advanced Management Journal*, 74(2), 32-41.

Zill, N., & Robinson, J. (1997, April). The Generation X difference. American Demographics, 17(4). 24.

Author Bio

Remi Alapo ("Dr. Remi") received her Doctorate from the University of Phoenix, Arizona in Organizational Management and Leadership in February 2011. She is currently an independent researcher with Global Management Consulting. Her research interests include international and cross-cultural management issues in Africa and other regions, especially with women's leadership. Specifically, she has projects on gender, decision-making, and emerging leader's perspectives on management geography, especially in areas of how national culture affects leaders' abilities to manage cross-culturally in international organizations.

Dr. Remi is also the Director of the Institute for Peace and Transformational Leadership (IPTL), an organization dedicated to her activities and interests in human rights, gender, and social justice. She previously taught Business Ethics and Social Responsibility while also working with start-up business leaders in Port–Au-Prince and Jeremie, Haiti from 2007-2009 as part of a Service-Learning and mission work.

Originally from Nigeria, Dr. Remi serves as an NGO United Nations Representative for the Women's Consortium of Nigeria (WOCON) and as a member of the African Women's Caucus of the Commission of the Status of Women (CSW) at the UN. A former member of the NGO Working Group on Women, Peace and Security—which monitored the UNSC Res. 1325 by UN member states. She has management and leadership experiences spanning over a 15 year period as the Managing Director of MEMI International—working with women business owners around the New York Metro area helping to improve their organizational effectiveness and business leadership.

Dr. Remi's experiences also span working and collaborating with those in leadership positions and observing some of the challenges of cross–cultural leadership and some ways in which many women in the Generation X group who are not able to attain the proper leadership positions because of not understanding how to effectively tackle organizational dynamics or societal misfits present in their immediate environment.

Generation X: The Role of Culture on the Leadership Styles of Women in Leadership Positions is Dr. Remi's first book on women and leadership. She is available for consultation to grassroots organizations and to women-owned business organizations looking to improve their management, leadership, and decision-making.

Dr. Remi can be contacted on her social media fan page: https://www.facebook.com/dr.remialapo/

APPENDIX

Frequency Tables

Age Group

		Frequency	Percent	Valid Percent	Cumulative Percent
Valid	30-34	13	43.3	43.3	43.3
	35-39	10	33.3	33.3	76.7
	40-44	2	6.7	6.7	83.3
	45 and Over	5	16.7	16.7	100.0
	Total	30	100.0	100.0	

Region of Origin

		Frequency	Percent	Valid Percent	Cumulative Percent
Valid	North-Central	7	23.3	23.3	23.3
	South-South	4	13.3	13.3	36.7
	South-East	9	30.0	30.0	66.7
	South-West	10	33.3	33.3	100.0
	Total	30	100.0	100.0	

137

Ethnic Group

		Frequency	Percent	Valid Percent	Cumulative Percent
Valid	Ibo	9	30.0	30.0	30.0
	Ibibio	1	3.3	3.3	33.3
	Yoruba	10	33.3	33.3	66.7
	Igala	1	3.3	3.3	70.0
	Igede	2	6.7	6.7	76.7
	Tiv	3	10.0	10.0	86.7
	Ebira	1	3.3	3.3	90.0
	Urhobo	1	3.3	3.3	93.3
	Efik	1	3.3	3.3	96.7
	Edo	1	3.3	3.3	100.0
	Total	30	100.0	100.0	

Highest Education Level

		Frequency	Percent	Valid Percent	Cumulative Percent
Valid	Bachelor	12	40.0	40.0	40.0
	Master's	13	43.3	43.3	83.3
	Doctorate	1	3.3	3.3	86.7
	Other	4	13.3	13.3	100.0
	Total	30	100.0	100.0	

138

Current Position in Organization

		Frequency	Percent	Valid Percent	Cumulative Percent
Valid	Management	12	40.0	40.0	40.0
	Executive	2	6.7	6.7	46.7
	Partner	1	3.3	3.3	50.0
	Owner	5	16.7	16.7	66.7
	Associate	9	30.0	30.0	96.7
	Snr Associate	1	3.3	3.3	100.0
	Total	30	100.0	100.0	

Years in Leadership Position

		Frequency	Percent	Valid Percent	Cumulative Percent
Valid	1-5 years	19	63.3	63.3	63.3
	6-10 years	7	23.3	23.3	86.7
	7-14 years	2	6.7	6.7	93.3
	15-20 years	1	3.3	3.3	96.7
	Over 20 years	1	3.3	3.3	100.0
	Total	30	100.0	100.0	

Number of People Managed

		Frequency	Percent	Valid Percent	Cumulative Percent
Valid	1-5	14	46.7	46.7	46.7
	6-10	8	26.7	26.7	73.3
	7-14	1	3.3	3.3	76.7
	15-20	2	6.7	6.7	83.3
	Over 20 people	5	16.7	16.7	100.0
	Total	30	100.0	100.0	

Annual Salary Range in USD

		Frequency	Percent	Valid Percent	Cumulative Percent
Valid	Under $25,000	11	36.7	36.7	36.7
	$25,001-$40,000	5	16.7	16.7	53.3
	$40,001-$55,000	3	10.0	10.0	63.3
	Over $55,001	11	36.7	36.7	100.0
	Total	30	100.0	100.0	

Religious Background

		Frequency	Percent	Valid Percent	Cumulative Percent
Valid	Christian	30	100.0	100.0	100.0

Economic Family Level

		Frequency	Percent	Valid Percent	Cumulative Percent
Valid	Upper Class	2	6.7	6.7	6.7
	Middle Class	28	93.3	93.3	100.0
	Total	30	100.0	100.0	

Leadership & Decision Making Style

		Frequency	Percent	Valid Percent	Cumulative Percent
Valid	Bureaucratic	1	3.3	3.3	3.3
	Democratic	13	43.3	43.3	46.7
	Situational	7	23.3	23.3	70.0
	Transformational	9	30.0	30.0	100.0
	Total	30	100.0	100.0	

Bar Charts

Region of Origin

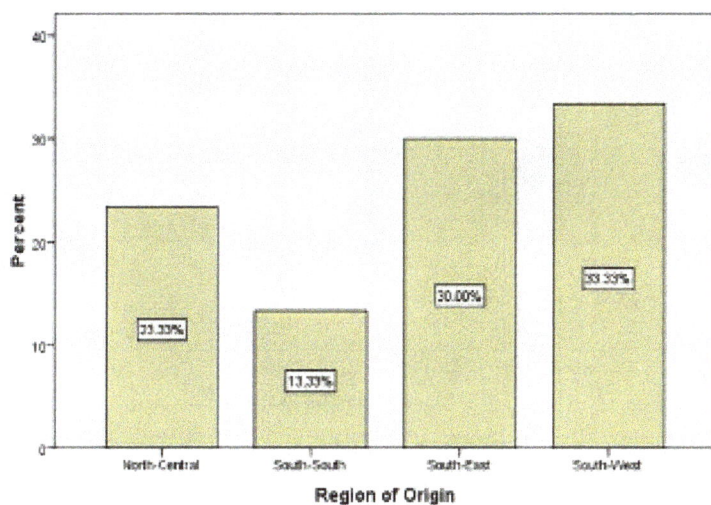

Ethnic Group

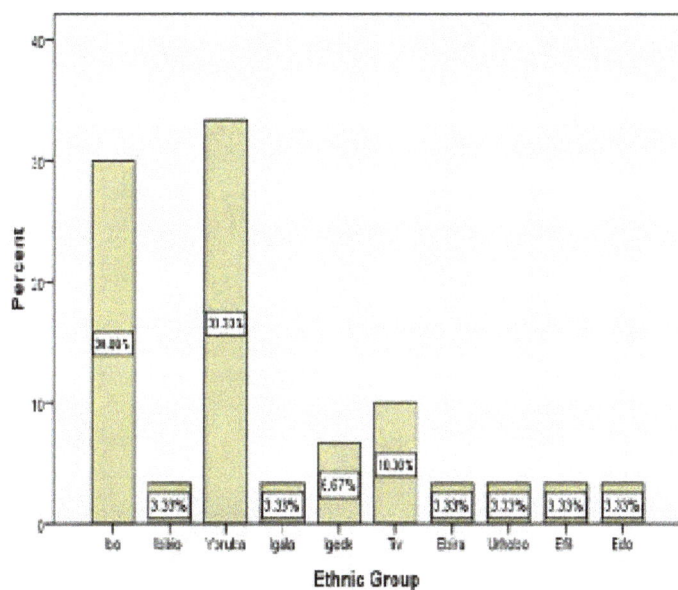

Highest Education Level

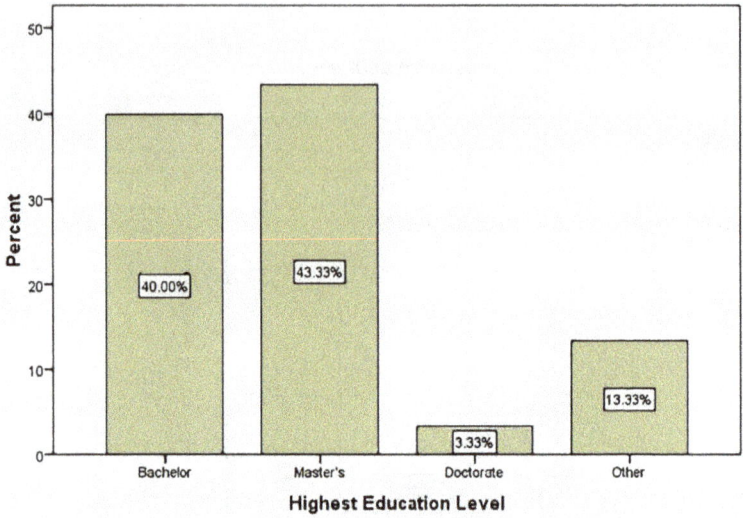

Highest Education Level

Current Position in Organization

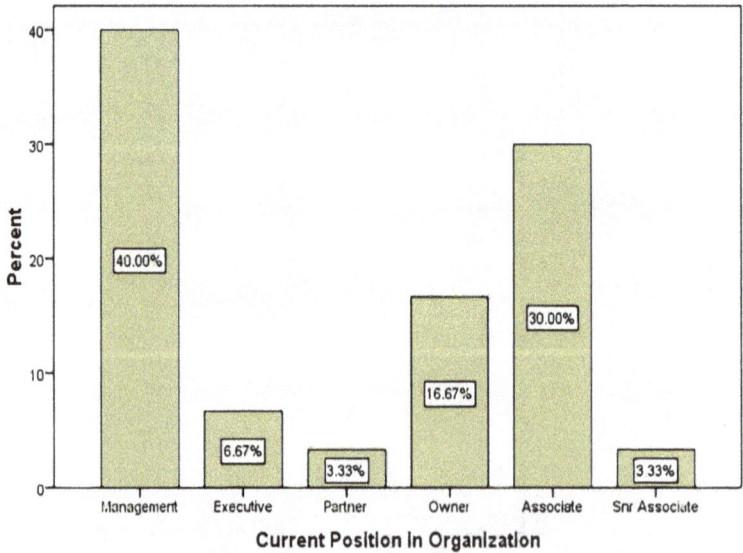

Current Position in Organization

Held of Leadership Position

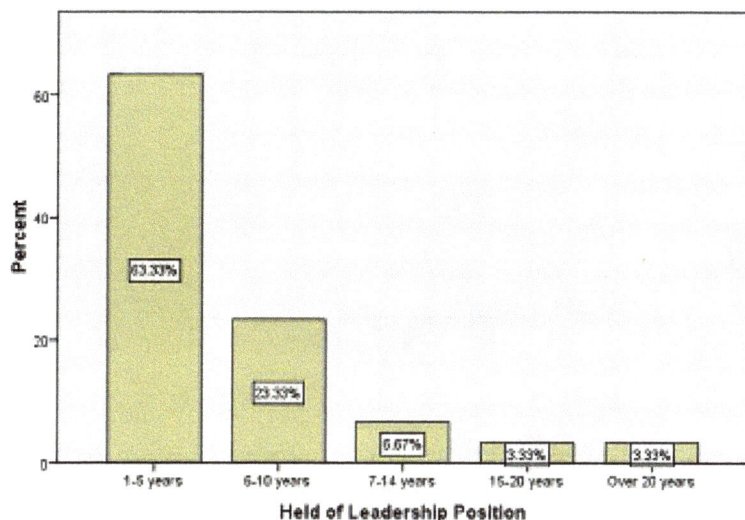

Percent (y-axis)

- 1-5 years: 63.33%
- 6-10 years: 23.33%
- 7-14 years: 6.67%
- 15-20 years: 3.33%
- Over 20 years: 3.33%

Held of Leadership Position (x-axis)

Number of People Managed

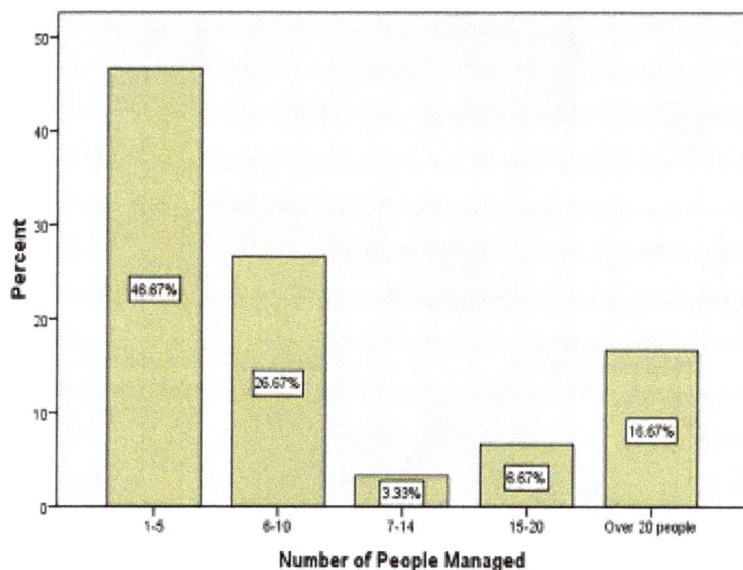

Percent (y-axis)

- 1-5: 46.67%
- 6-10: 26.67%
- 7-14: 3.33%
- 15-20: 6.67%
- Over 20 people: 16.67%

Number of People Managed (x-axis)

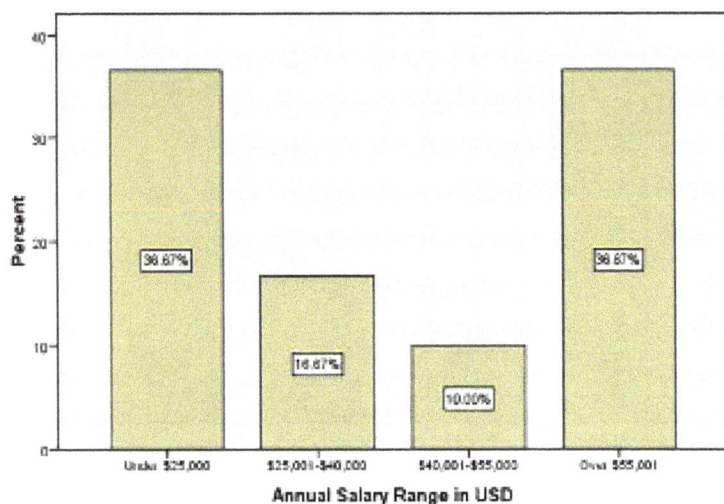

Annual Salary Range in USD

Under $25,000: 36.67%
$25,001-$40,000: 16.67%
$40,001-$55,000: 10.00%
Over $55,001: 36.67%

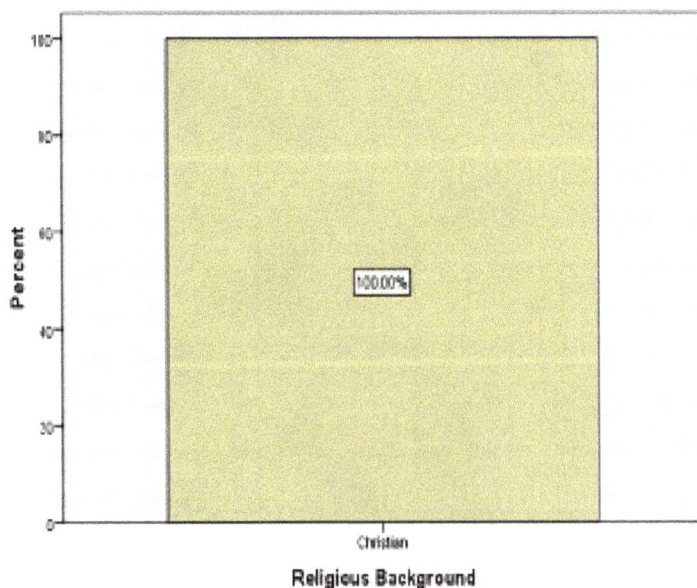

Religious Background

Christian: 100.00%

Economic Family Level

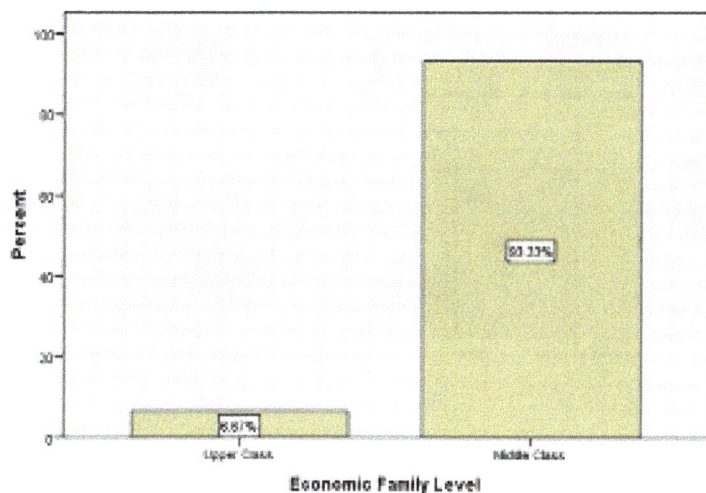

Leadership & Decision Making Style

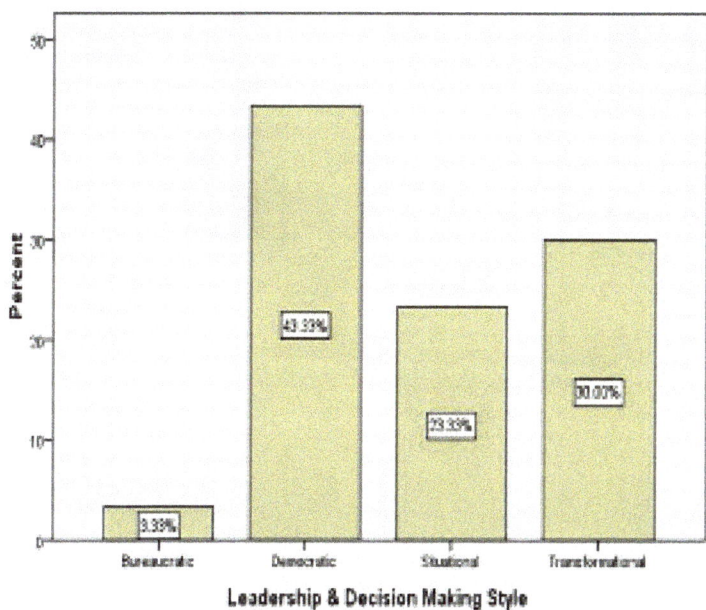

145

Crosstabs

Age Group * Region of Origin Crosstabulation

Count

		Region of Origin				
		North-Central	South-South	South-East	South-West	Total
Age Group	30-34	3	1	4	5	13
	35-39	3	3	4	0	10
	40-44	1	0	0	1	2
	45 and Over	0	0	1	4	5
	Total	7	4	9	10	30

Bar Chart

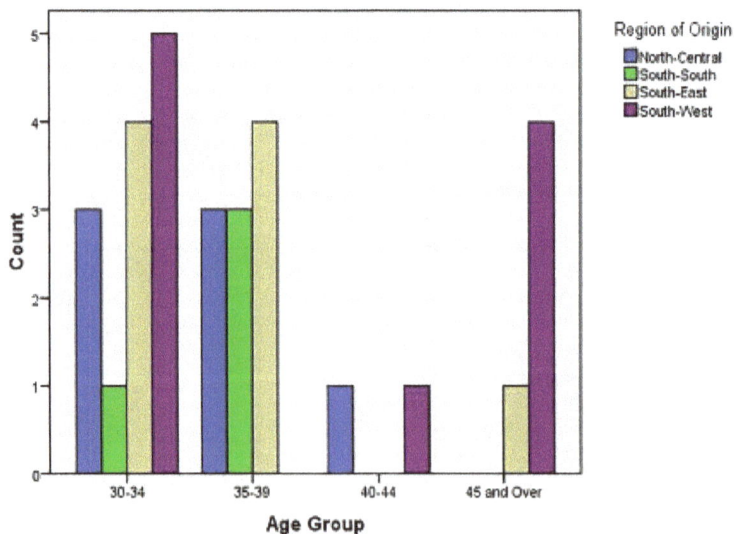

Age Group * Ethnic Group Crosstabulation

Count

		Ethnic Group					
		Ibo	Ibibio	Yoruba	Igala	Igede	Tiv
Age Group	30-34	4	0	5	1	1	1
	35-39	4	1	0	0	1	2
	40-44	0	0	1	0	0	0
	45 and Over	1	0	4	0	0	0
	Total	9	1	10	1	2	3

Age. Group * Ethnic Group Crosstabulation

Count

		Ethnic Group				Total
		Ebira	Urhobo	Efik	Edo	
Age Group	30-34	0	1	0	0	13
	35-39	0	0	1	1	10
	40-44	1	0	0	0	2
	45 and Over	0	0	0	0	5
	Total	1	1	1	1	30

Bar Chart

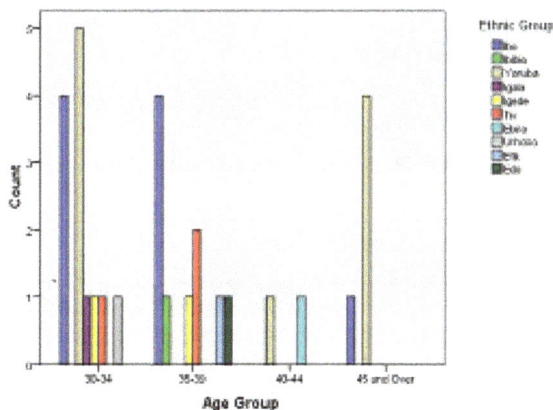

Age Group * Highest Education Level Crosstabulation

Count

		\multicolumn{4}{c}{Highest Education Level}	Total
		Bachelor	Master's	Doctorate	Other	Total
Age Group	30-34	3	10	0	0	13
	35-39	7	1	0	2	10
	40-44	0	2	0	0	2
	45 and Over	2	0	1	2	5
	Total	12	13	1	4	30

Bar Chart

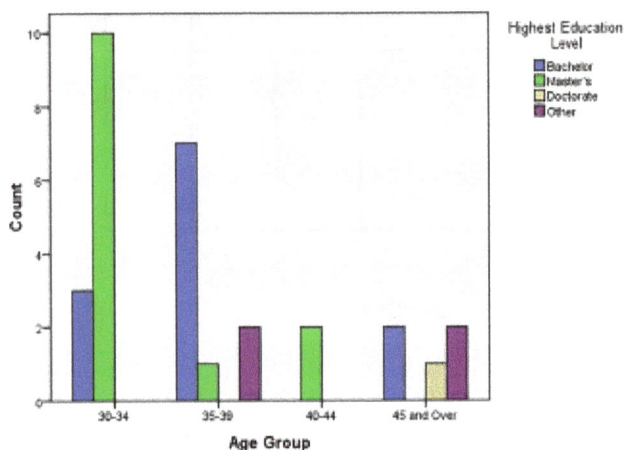

Age Group * Current Position in Organization Crosstabulation

Count

		\multicolumn{5}{c}{Current Position in Organization}
		Management	Executive	Partner	Owner	Associate
Age Group	30-34	5	0	0	1	6
	35-39	3	1	1	4	1
	40-44	1	0	0	0	1
	45 and Over	3	1	0	0	1
	Total	12	2	1	5	9

Age Group * Current Position in Organization Crosstabulation

Count

		Current Position in Organization	
		Snr Associate	Total
Age Group	30-34	1	13
	35-39	0	10
	40-44	0	2
	45 and Over	0	5
	Total	1	30

Bar Chart

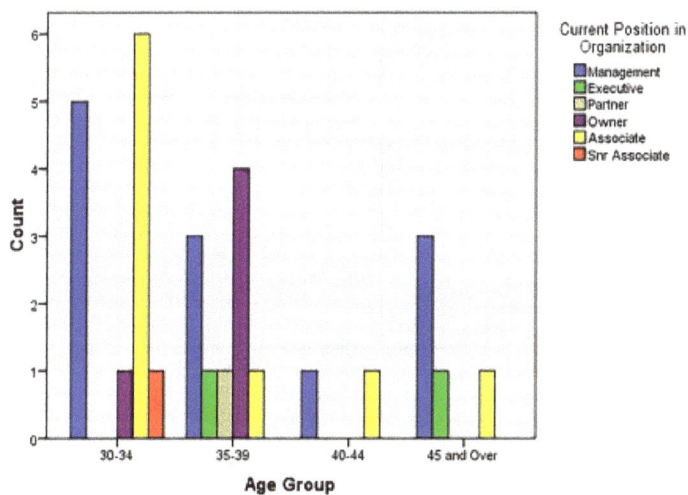

149

Age Group * Head of Leadership Position Crosstabulation

Count

		Held of Leadership Position			
		1-5 years	6-10 years	7-14 years	15-20 years
Age Group	30-34	12	1	0	0
	35-39	5	5	0	0
	40-44	2	0	0	0
	45 and Over	0	1	2	1
	Total	19	7	2	1

Age Group * Head of Leadership Position Crosstabulation

Count

		Held of Leadership Position	Total
		Over 20 years	
Age Group	30-34	0	13
	35-39	0	10
	40-44	0	2
	45 and Over	1	5
	Total	1	30

Bar Chart

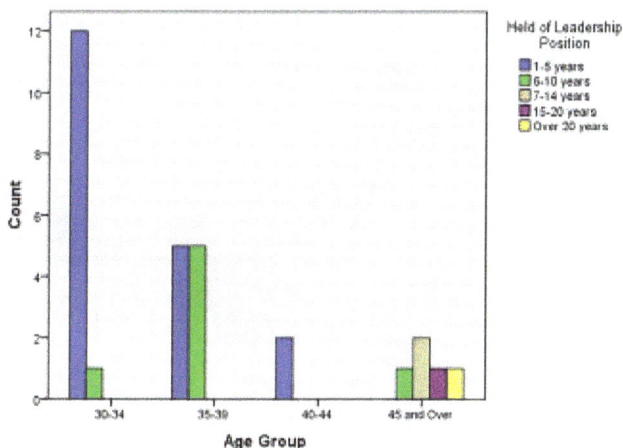

Held of Leadership Position
- 1-5 years
- 6-10 years
- 7-14 years
- 15-20 years
- Over 20 years

Age Group * Number of People Managed Crosstabulation

Count

		Number of People Managed					Total
		1-5	6-10	7-14	15-20	Over 20 people	
Age Group	30-34	7	3	0	1	2	13
	35-39	4	4	0	1	1	10
	40-44	2	0	0	0	0	2
	45 and Over	1	1	1	0	2	5
	Total	14	8	1	2	5	30

Bar Chart

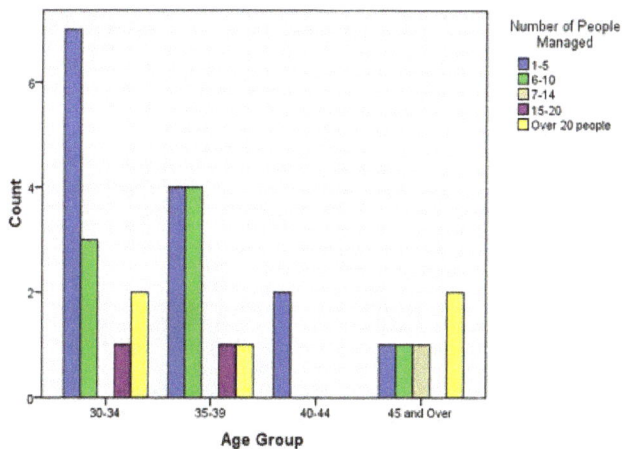

Number of People Managed
- 1-5
- 6-10
- 7-14
- 15-20
- Over 20 people

Age Group * Annual Salary Range in USD Crosstabulation

Count

		Annual Salary Range in USD				Total
		Under $25,000	$25,001-$40,000	$40,001-$55,000	Over $55,001	
Age Group	30-34	3	4	2	4	13
	35-39	6	1	0	3	10
	40-44	1	0	0	1	2
	45 and Over	1	0	1	3	5
	Total	11	5	3	11	30

Bar Chart

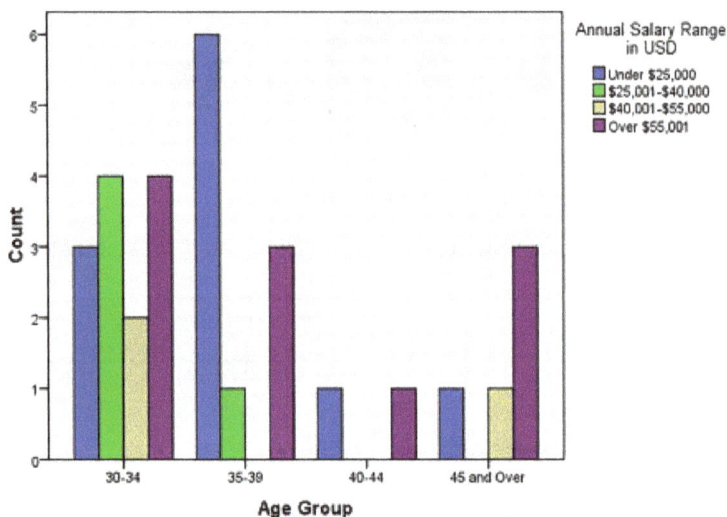

Age Group * Religious Background Crosstabulation

Count

		Religious Background	Total
		Christian	
Age Group	30-34	13	13
	35-39	10	10
	40-44	2	2
	45 and Over	5	5
	Total	30	30

Bar Chart

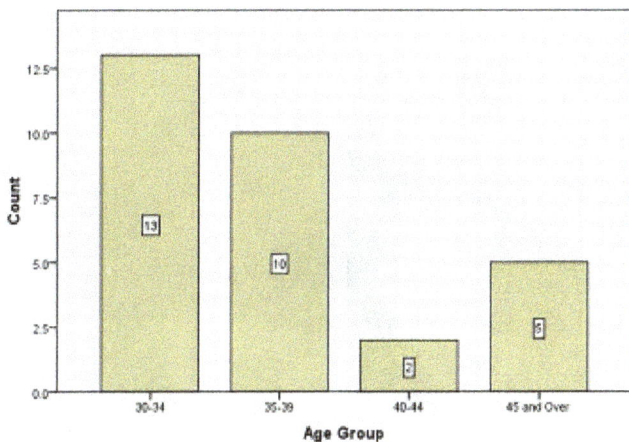

Age Group * Economic Family Level Crosstabulation

Count

		Economic Family Level		
		Upper Class	Middle Class	Total
Age Group	30-34	0	13	13
	35-39	1	9	10
	40-44	0	2	2
	45 and Over	1	4	5
	Total	2	28	30

Bar Chart

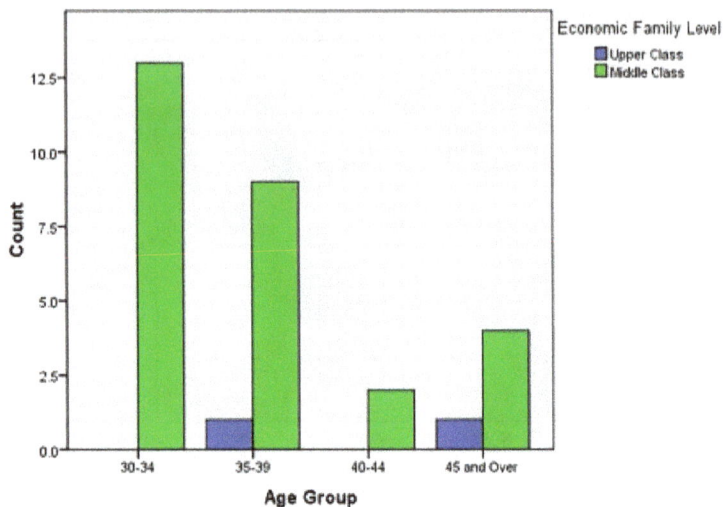

Age Group * Leadership & Decision-Making Style Crosstabulation

Count

		Leadership & Decision Making Style				Total
		Bureaucratic	Democratic	Situational	Transformational	
Age Group	30-34	0	5	3	5	13
	35-39	1	3	4	2	10
	40-44	0	2	0	0	2
	45 and Over	0	3	0	2	5
	Total	1	13	7	9	30

Bar Chart

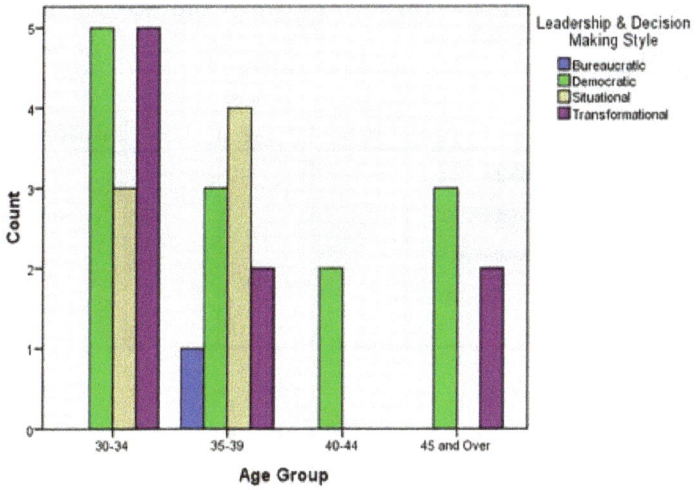

Crosstabs

Region of Origin * Age Group Crosstabulation

Count

		Age Group				Total
		30-34	35-39	40-44	45 and Over	
Region of Origin	North-Central	3	3	1	0	7
	South-South	1	3	0	0	4
	South-East	4	4	0	1	9
	South-West	5	0	1	4	10
	Total	13	10	2	5	30

Bar Chart

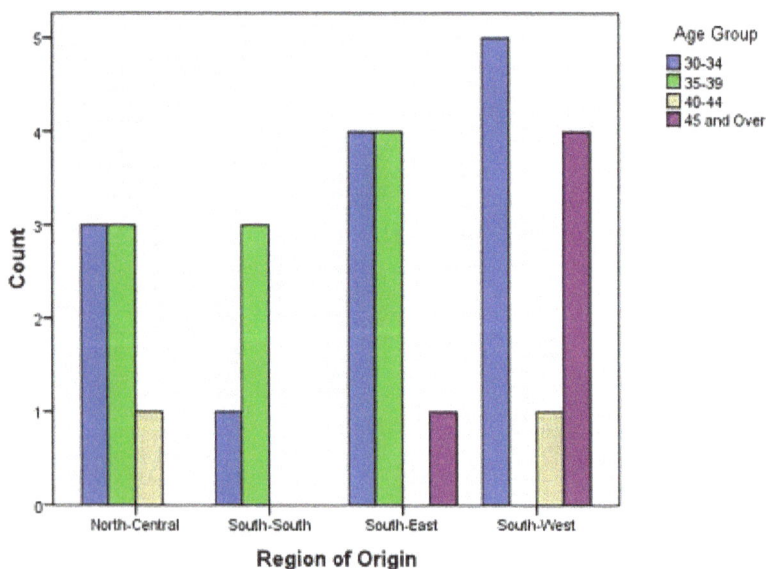

Ethnic Group * Age Group Crosstabulation

Count

		Age Group				Total
		30-34	35-39	40-44	45 and Over	
Ethnic Group	Ibo	4	4	0	1	9
	Ibibio	0	1	0	0	1
	Yoruba	5	0	1	4	10
	Igala	1	0	0	0	1
	Igede	1	1	0	0	2
	Tiv	1	2	0	0	3
	Ebira	0	0	1	0	1
	Urhobo	1	0	0	0	1
	Efik	0	1	0	0	1
	Edo	0	1	0	0	1
	Total	13	10	2	5	30

Bar Chart

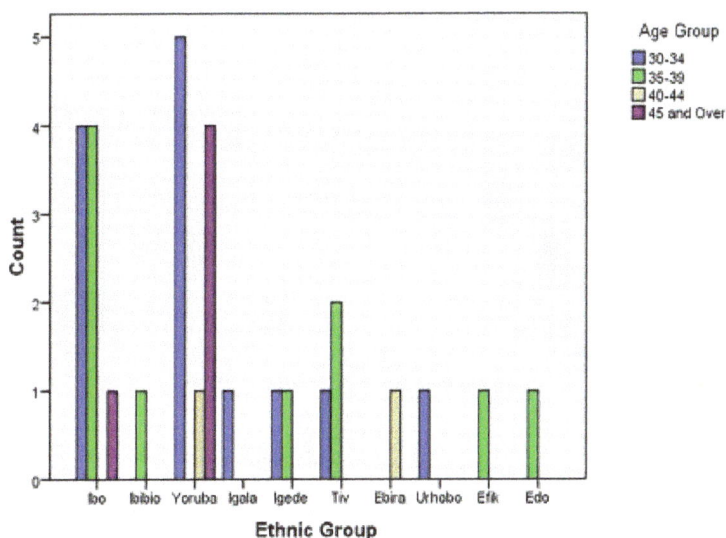

Highest Education Level * Age Group Crosstabulation

Count

		Age Group				Total
		30-34	35-39	40-44	45 and Over	
Highest Education Level	Bachelor	3	7	0	2	12
	Master's	10	1	2	0	13
	Doctorate	0	0	0	1	1
	Other	0	2	0	2	4
	Total	13	10	2	5	30

Bar Chart

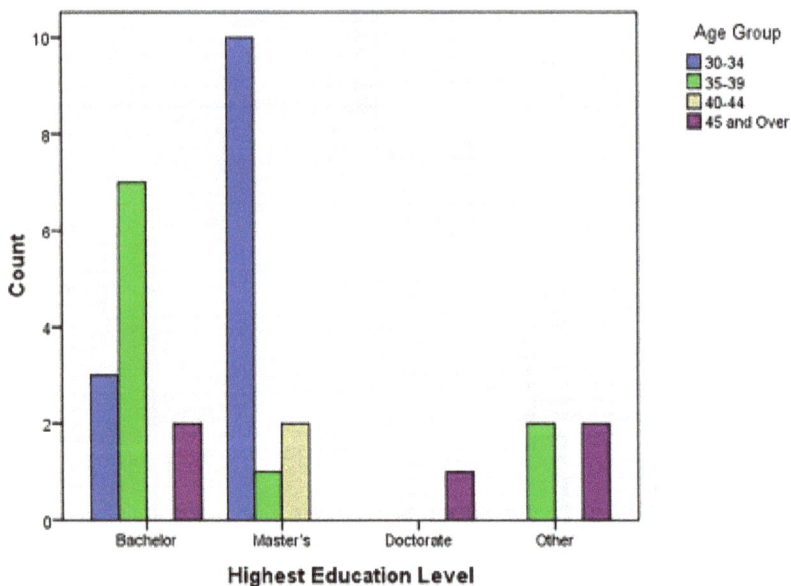

Current Position in Organization * Age Group Crosstabulation

Current Position in Organization * Age Group Cross tabulation

Count

		Age Group				Total
		30-34	35-39	40-44	45 and Over	
Current Position in Organization	Management	5	3	1	3	12
	Executive	0	1	0	1	2
	Partner	0	1	0	0	1
	Owner	1	4	0	0	5
	Associate	6	1	1	1	9
	Snr Associate	1	0	0	0	1
	Total	13	10	2	5	30

Bar Chart

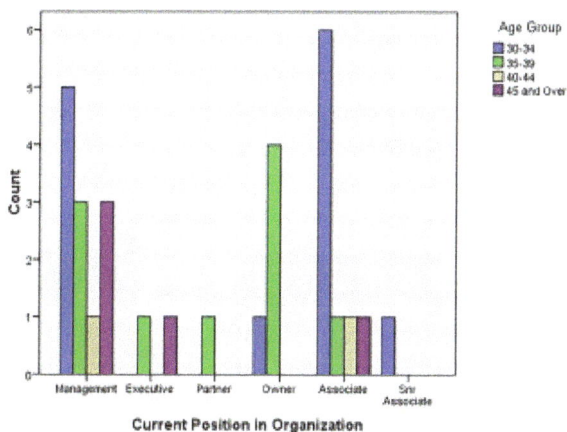

159

Held of Leadership Position * Age Group Crosstabulation

Count

		Age Group				Total
		30-34	35-39	40-44	45 and Over	
Held of Leadership Position	1-5 years	12	5	2	0	19
	6-10 years	1	5	0	1	7
	7-14 years	0	0	0	2	2
	15-20 years	0	0	0	1	1
	Over 20 years	0	0	0	1	1
	Total	13	10	2	5	30

Bar Chart

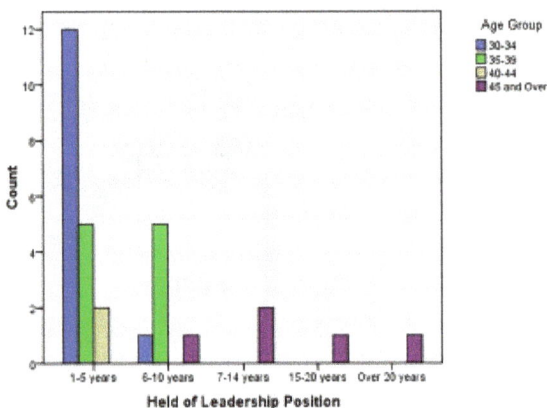

Number of People Managed * Age Group Crosstabulation

Count

		Age Group				Total
		30-34	35-39	40-44	45 and Over	
Number of People Managed	1-5	7	4	2	1	14
	6-10	3	4	0	1	8
	7-14	0	0	0	1	1
	15-20	1	1	0	0	2
	Over 20 people	2	1	0	2	5
	Total	13	10	2	5	30

Bar Chart

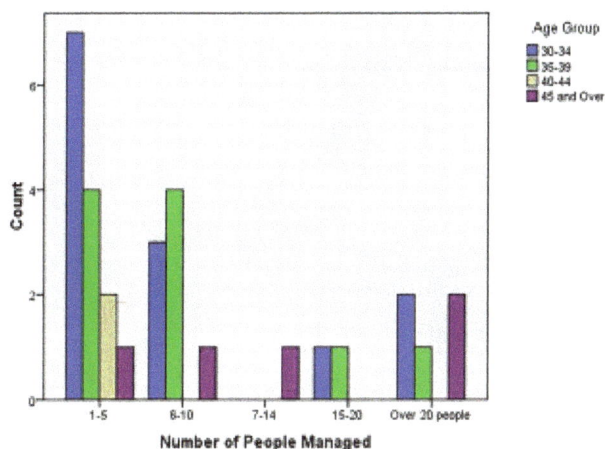

Annual Salary Range in USD * Age Group Crosstabulation

Count

		Age Group		
		30-34	35-39	40-44
Annual Salary Range in USD	Under $25,000	3	6	1
	$25,001-$40,000	4	1	0
	$40,001-$55,000	2	0	0
	Over $55,001	4	3	1
	Total	13	10	2

Annual Salary Range in USD * Age Group Crosstabulation

Count

		Age Group	
		45 and Over	Total
Annual Salary Range in USD	Under $25,000	1	11
	$25,001-$40,000	0	5
	$40,001-$55,000	1	3
	Over $55,001	3	11
	Total	5	30

Bar Chart

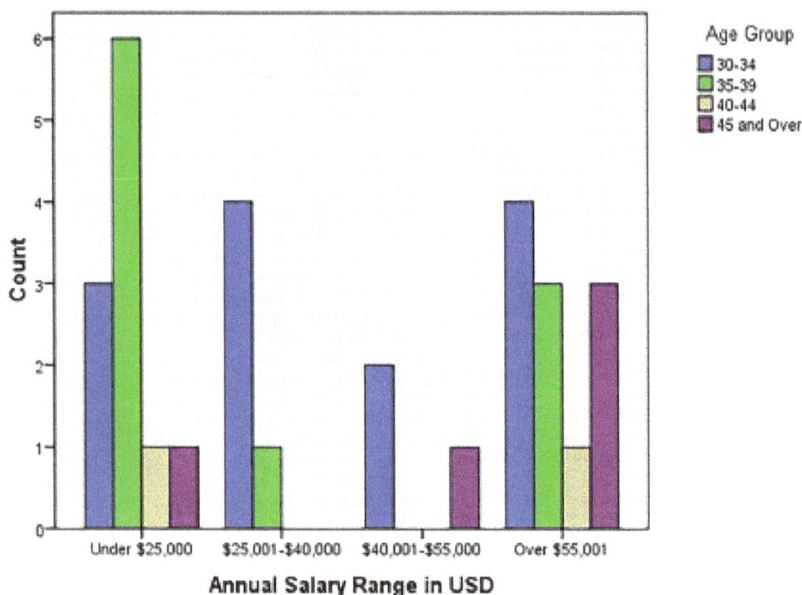

Religious Background * Age Group Crosstabulation

Count

		Age Group				
		30-34	35-39	40-44	45 and Over	Total
Religious Background	Christian	13	10	2	5	30
	Total	13	10	2	5	30

Bar Chart

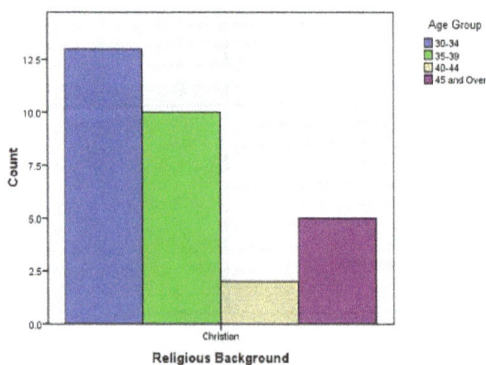

162

Economic Family Level * Age Group Crosstabulation

Count

		Age Group				Total
		30-34	35-39	40-44	45 and Over	
Economic Family Level	Upper Class	0	1	0	1	2
	Middle Class	13	9	2	4	28
	Total	13	10	2	5	30

Bar Chart

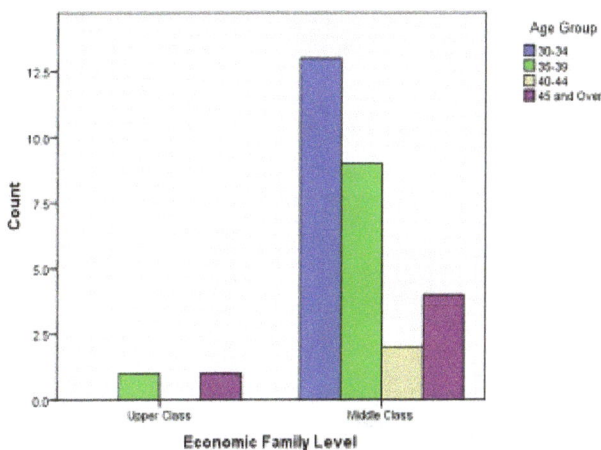

Leadership & Decision-Making Style * Age Group Crosstabulation

Count

		Age Group		
		30-34	35-39	40-44
Leadership & Decision Making Style	Bureaucratic	0	1	0
	Democratic	5	3	2
	Situational	3	4	0
	Transformational	5	2	0
	Total	13	10	2

Leadership & Decision-Making Style * Age Group Crosstabulation

Count

		Age Group	
		45 and Over	Total
Leadership & Decision Making Style	Bureaucratic	0	1
	Democratic	3	13
	Situational	0	7
	Transformational	2	9
	Total	5	30

Bar Chart

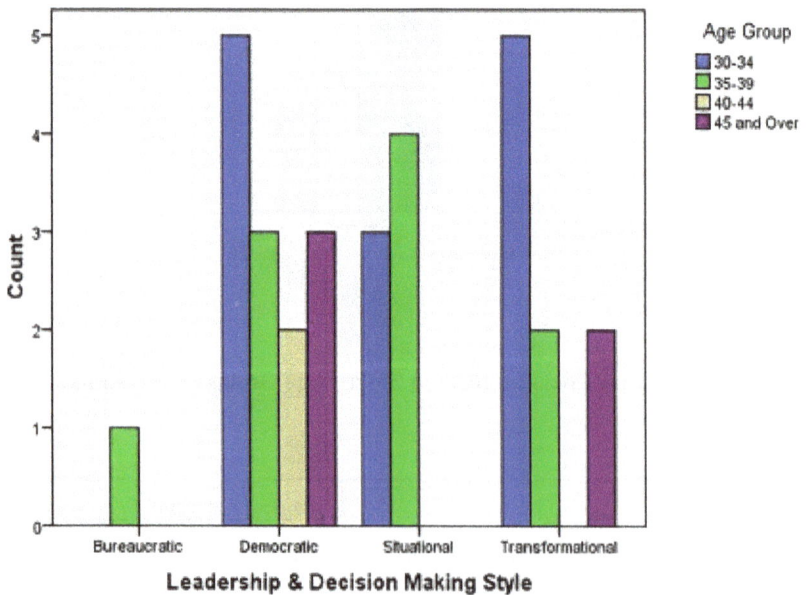

Leadership & Decision Making Style

Age Group
- 30-34
- 35-39
- 40-44
- 45 and Over

Region of Origin * Leadership & Decision-Making Style Crosstabulation

Count

		Leadership & Decision Making Style				Total
		Bureaucratic	Democratic	Situational	Transformational	
Region of Origin	North-Central	0	2	3	2	7
	South-South	1	1	1	1	4
	South-East	0	4	2	3	9
	South-West	0	6	1	3	10
	Total	1	13	7	9	30

Bar Chart

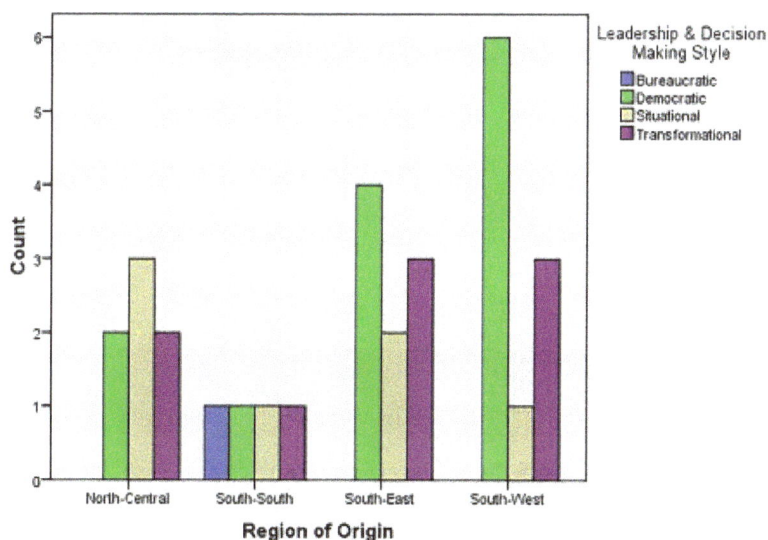

165

Crosstabs

Region of Origin * Leadership & Decision-Making Style Crosstabulation

Count

		Leadership & Decision Making Style				
		Bureaucratic	Democratic	Situational	Transformational	Total
Region of Origin	North-Central	0	2	3	2	7
	South-South	1	1	1	1	4
	South-East	0	4	2	3	9
	South-West	0	6	1	3	10
	Total	1	13	7	9	30

Bar Chart

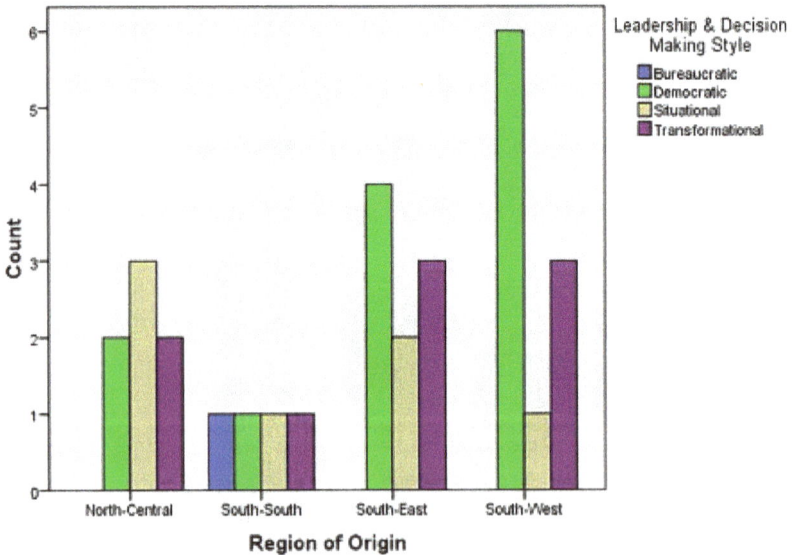

166

Ethnic Group * Leadership & Decision-Making Style Crosstabulation

Count

		Leadership & Decision Making Style				Total
		Bureaucratic	Democratic	Situational	Transformational	
Ethnic Group	Ibo	0	4	2	3	9
	Ibibio	0	0	0	1	1
	Yoruba	0	6	1	3	10
	Igala	0	0	0	1	1
	Igede	0	1	1	0	2
	Tiv	0	0	2	1	3
	Ebira	0	1	0	0	1
	Urhobo	0	1	0	0	1
	Efik	1	0	0	0	1
	Edo	0	0	1	0	1
	Total	1	13	7	9	30

Bar Chart

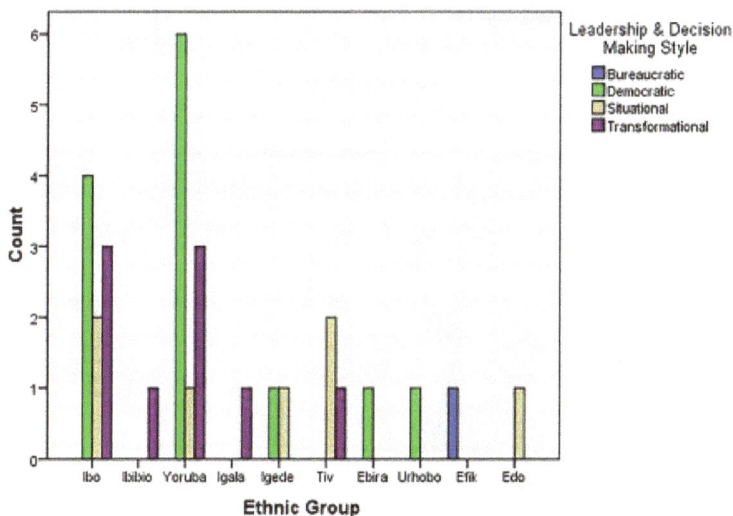

Highest Education Level * Leadership & Decision-Making Style Crosstabulation

Count

		Leadership & Decision Making Style		
		Bureaucratic	Democratic	Situational
Highest Education Level	Bachelor	1	3	4
	Master's	0	7	2
	Doctorate	0	0	0
	Other	0	3	1
	Total	1	13	7

Highest Education Level * Leadership & Decision-Making Style Crosstabulation

Count

		Leadership & Decision Making Style	
		Transformational	Total
Highest Education Level	Bachelor	4	12
	Master's	4	13
	Doctorate	1	1
	Other	0	4
	Total	9	30

Bar Chart

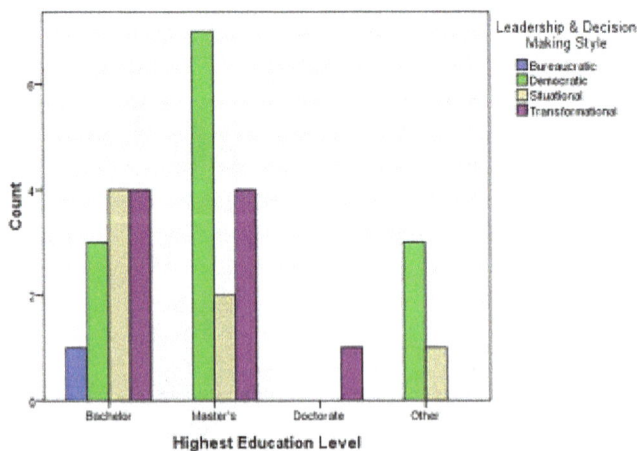

Current Position in Organization * Leadership & Decision-Making Style Crosstabulation

Count

		Leadership & Decision Making Style		
		Bureaucratic	Democratic	Situational
Current Position in Organization	Management	0	7	2
	Executive	0	0	1
	Partner	0	0	0
	Owner	1	2	1
	Associate	0	3	3
	Snr Associate	0	1	0
	Total	1	13	7

Current Position in Organization * Leadership & Decision-Making Style Crosstabulation

Count

		Leadership & Decision Making Style	Total
		Transformational	
Current Position in Organization	Management	3	12
	Executive	1	2
	Partner	1	1
	Owner	1	5
	Associate	3	9
	Snr Associate	0	1
	Total	9	30

Bar Chart

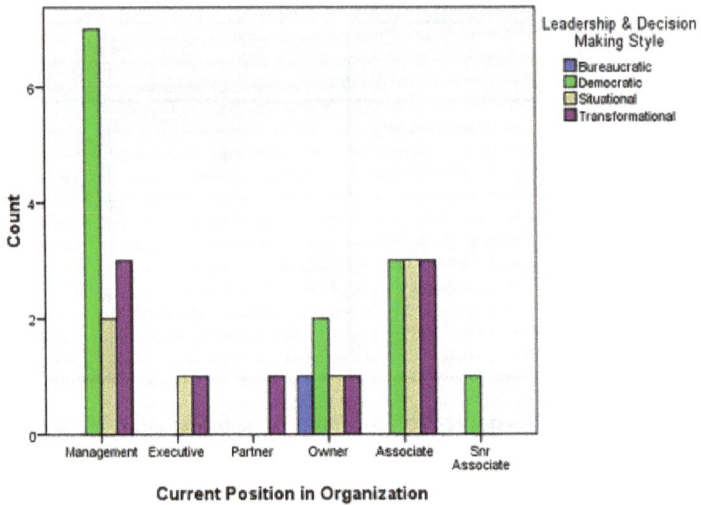

Current Position in Organization

Held of Leadership Position * Leadership & Decision-Making Style Crosstabulation

Count

		Leadership & Decision Making Style		
		Bureaucratic	Democratic	Situational
Held of Leadership Position	1-5 years	0	9	4
	6-10 years	1	1	3
	7-14 years	0	2	0
	15-20 years	0	0	0
	Over 20 years	0	1	0
	Total	1	13	7

Held of Leadership Position * Leadership & Decision-Making Style Crosstabulation

Count

		Leadership & Decision Making Style	
		Transformational	Total
Held of Leadership Position	1-5 years	6	19
	6-10 years	2	7
	7-14 years	0	2
	15-20 years	1	1
	Over 20 years	0	1
	Total	9	30

Bar Chart

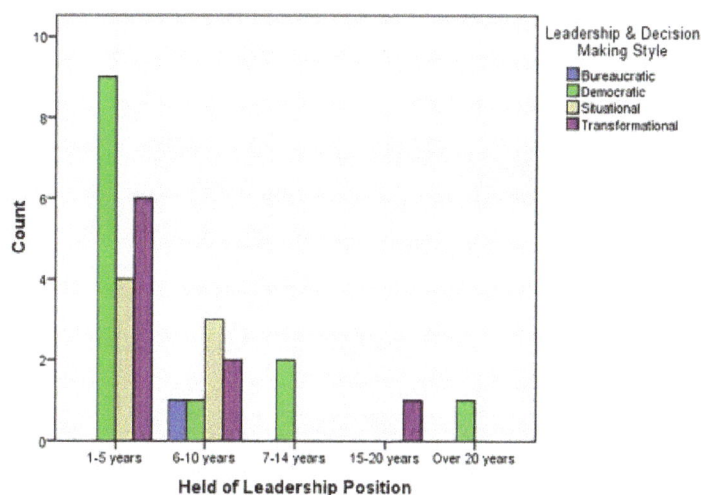

Number of People Managed * Leadership & Decision-Making Style Crosstabulation

Count

		Leadership & Decision Making Style		
		Bureaucratic	Democratic	Situational
Number of People Managed	1-5	1	7	2
	6-10	0	2	3
	7-14	0	1	0
	15-20	0	1	1
	Over 20 people	0	2	1
	Total	1	13	7

Number of People Managed * Leadership & Decision-Making Style Crosstabulation

Count

		Leadership & Decision Making Style	
		Transformational	Total
Number of People Managed	1-5	4	14
	6-10	3	8
	7-14	0	1
	15-20	0	2
	Over 20 people	2	5
	Total	9	30

Bar Chart

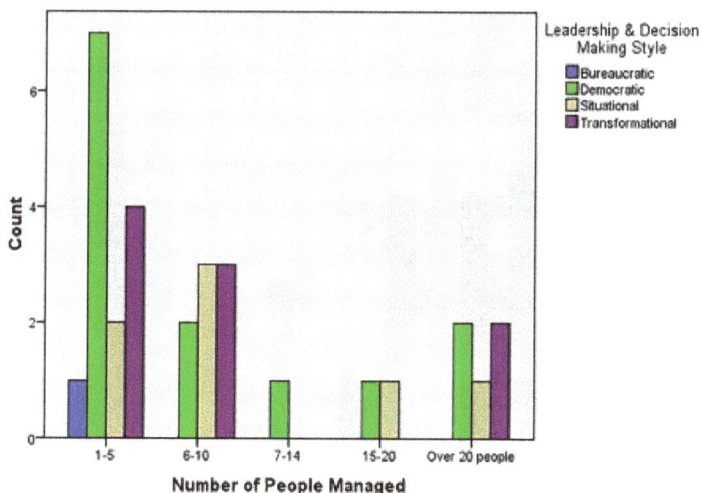

Annual Salary Range in USD * Leadership & Decision-Making Style Crosstabulation

Count

		Leadership & Decision Making Style		
		Bureaucratic	Democratic	Situational
Annual Salary Range in USD	Under $25,000	1	4	3
	$25,001-$40,000	0	3	1
	$40,001-$55,000	0	2	1
	Over $55,001	0	4	2
	Total	1	13	7

Annual Salary Range in USD * Leadership & Decision-Making Style Crosstabulation

Count

		Leadership & Decision Making Style	
		Transformational	Total
Annual Salary Range in USD	Under $25,000	3	11
	$25,001-$40,000	1	5
	$40,001-$55,000	0	3
	Over $55,001	5	11
	Total	9	30

Bar Chart

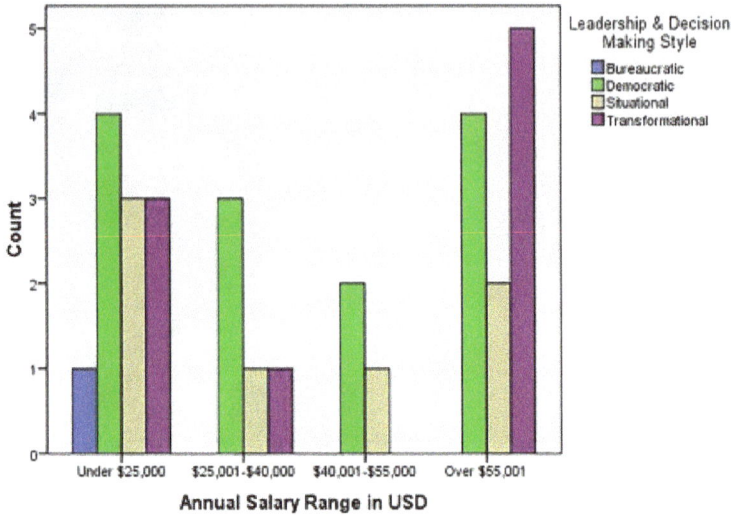

Religious Background * Leadership & Decision-Making Style Crosstabulation

Count

		Leadership & Decision Making Style				
		Bureaucratic	Democratic	Situational	Transformational	Total
Religious Background	Christian	1	13	7	9	30
	Total	1	13	7	9	30

Bar Chart

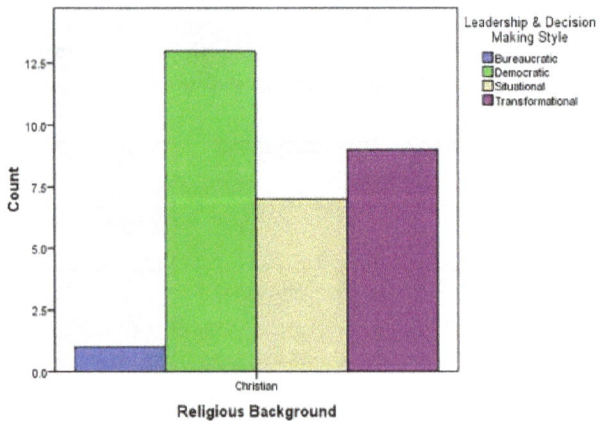

174

Economic Family Level * Leadership & Decision-Making Style Crosstabulation

Count

		Leadership & Decision Making Style		
		Bureaucratic	Democratic	Situational
Economic Family Level	Upper Class	0	0	1
	Middle Class	1	13	6
	Total	1	13	7

Economic Family Level * Leadership & Decision-Making Style Crosstabulation

Count

		Leadership & Decision Making Style	
		Transformational	Total
Economic Family Level	Upper Class	1	2
	Middle Class	8	28
	Total	9	30

Bar Chart

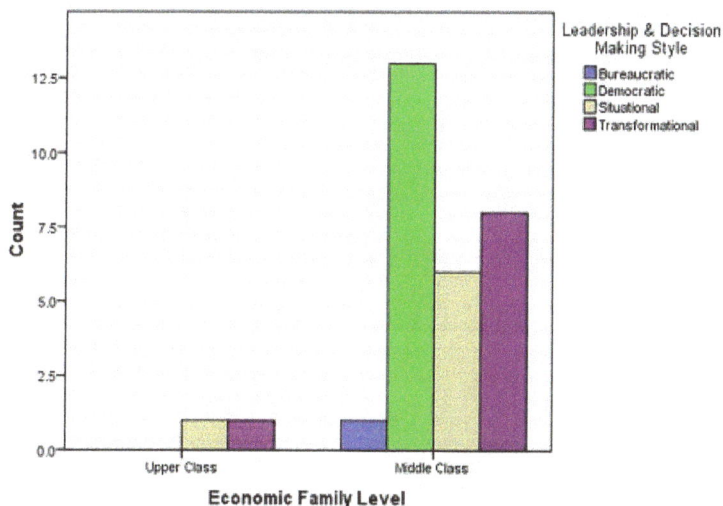

KEYWORDS

The following keywords resonated from the descriptive outcomes of the study found on pages 68-98. These are not a complete set of keywords described by participants as some of the challenges they may be facing as Generation X women in Leadership positions leading in a 21st-century global landscape. These keywords are included in the appendix even though the outcomes have been presented in the different figures found on each of the descriptive outcomes from the questionnaire. The rest of the data have been included in the appendix section to give readers a more in-depth understanding of the rest of the data that was gathered and analyzed.

1. **Obstacles Encountered**

- Prescribed role
- Need to work harder
- Young age
- Maternity
- Disciplinary challenges

2. **View of Power**

- Knowledgeable
- Advanced skills
- Recognition
- Personal conviction
- Going the extra mile
- Responsibility
- Integrity
- Ability to control challenges
- Leading positively
- Opportunity to lead
- Make rules
- Punish rightly within the organization

3. Treatment by Peers

- Skepticism
- Confrontational
- Judgmental
- Helpful
- Divided
- Supportive
- Cooperative
- Helpful

4. Asset of the Use of Power

- Ability to take responsibility
- Professionalism
- Build trust and relationships
- Active listening
- Role model
- Establish long and short term vision and goals

5. Generation X and Power

- Independence
- Self – confidence
- Financially stable
- Opportunity to live in a diverse and multi-cultural environment
- Exposure to new technology
- Breaking of some cultural norms and barriers which set women backwards

6. Role of National and Family Culture

- Natural tendency of assigned family roles
- A tool that helped to nurture women's potentials
- Dynamic and transitional shift of women in the economic and leadership ladder

- Importance of filial duties
- Need to break some obstacles – culture, national, family, gender disparity
- Both the family culture positive and negative

7. **Cultural values when exercising power**

- Regard for older generation
- Respect for people in higher positions

8. **Differences in leadership of previous generation**

   Baby Boomers:

   More submissive
   Sentimental on the maternal angle
   Tolerance
   Home makers
   Nurturers
   Laid back
   Intimidated due to societal culture

   Generation X:

   Independent
   Bold
   Audacious
   Broken glass ceiling

9. **Treatment by Previous Generation**

- Ambivalence
- Ignoring familial duties
- Misplaced priorities
- Too much independent
- Supportive

- Respectful

10. Effect of Demographics on the View of Power

- Career achievement
- Financial independent and stability
- Goal accomplishment
- Humble and not abuse power
- Afford leadership training courses
- Give back to society
- Respect
- Fairness to others
- Moral judgement
- Servant hood

11. Leadership and Decision-Making – attribute only, no key words

12. Reasons for Selecting Leadership Styles

Democratic

> Team work
> Sense of belonging
> Feeling of responsibility
> Collaborative decision-making
> More commitment
> Freedom of expression and ideas
> Problem solving without being looked down upon

Situational

> Adaptive measures
> Environmental Challenges
> Differences in culture
> Diverse perspectives

Social and economic status of subordinates
Business and organizational perspectives
Changing needs
Flexibility

Transformational
Team work
Inspire others
Give back to others
Motivate employees
Lasting impression on others
Lead by example
Mentoring
Encouragement
Personal examples and stories
Lasting change in lives

13. Day-to-Day Challenges

- Bureaucratic bottlenecks

14. Societal challenges

- Women are less corrupt
- Corrupt set up of the society

15. Styles of leadership varies

- Depends on situation

ATTRIBUTES TABLE

Table of Attributes

Id	Age	Region	Ethnic	EdLevel	Position	LeadPosition	NumManag	Salary	Religion	FamLevel	LeadStyle
1	35-39	South-East	Ibo	Bachelor	Management	6-10 years	15-20	Over $55,001	Christian	Middle Class	Situational
2	30-34	South-East	Ibo	Master's	Management	1-5 years	15-20	$25,001-$40,000	Christian	Middle Class	Democratic
3	35-39	South-East	Ibo	Other	Owner	1-5 years	1-5	$25,001-$40,000	Christian	Middle Class	Democratic
4	35-39	South-East	Ibo	Master's	Associate	1-5 years	Over 20 people	Under $25,000	Christian	Middle Class	Transformational
5	35-39	South-South	Ibibio	Bachelor	Partner	6-10 years	1-5	Over $55,001	Christian	Middle Class	Transformational
6	45 and Over	South-East	Yoruba	Bachelor	Management	7-14 years	7-14	$40,001-$55,000	Christian	Middle Class	Democratic
7	45 and Over	South-West	Yoruba	Bachelor	Executive	6-10 years	6-10	Over $55,001	Christian	Middle Class	Transformational
8	30-34	North-Central	Igala	Master's	Management	1-5 years	6-10	Under $25,000	Christian	Middle Class	Transformational
9	30-34	South-West	Yoruba	Master's	Associate	1-5 years	Over 20 people	$25,001-$40,000	Christian	Middle Class	Democratic
10	45 and Over	South-West	Yoruba	Other	Management	7-14 years	Over 20 people	Under $25,000	Christian	Middle Class	Democratic
11	30-34	South-West	Yoruba	Bachelor	Management	1-5 years	6-10	Over $55,001	Christian	Middle Class	Democratic
12	35-39	North-Central	Igede	Bachelor	Management	1-5 years	1-5	Over $55,001	Christian	Middle Class	Democratic
13	30-34	South-East	Ibo	Master's	Associate	1-5 years	1-5	$25,001-$40,000	Christian	Middle Class	Democratic
14	30-34	South-West	Yoruba	Bachelor	Management	1-5 years	1-5	Under $25,000	Christian	Middle Class	Transformational
15	30-34	South-East	Ibo	Master's	Management	1-5 years	6-10	Over $55,001	Christian	Middle Class	Transformational
16	30-34	North-Central	Tiv	Master's	Snr Associate	1-5 years	1-5	Over $55,001	Christian	Middle Class	Democratic
17	30-34	South-South	Igala	Master's	Associate	1-5 years	1-5	Over $55,001	Christian	Middle Class	Democratic
18	30-34	South-East	Ibo	Bachelor	Associate	1-5 years	1-5	Under $25,000	Christian	Middle Class	Situational
19	40-44	South-West	Yoruba	Master's	Management	1-5 years	1-5	Over $55,001	Christian	Middle Class	Democratic
20	35-39	North-Central	Tiv	Other	Executive	1-5 years	1-5	Over $55,001	Christian	Upper Class	Situational
21	30-34	South-West	Yoruba	Master's	Owner	1-5 years	1-5	Over $55,001	Christian	Middle Class	Transformational
22	45 and Over	South-West	Yoruba	Other	Management	Over 20 years	Over 20 people	Over $55,001	Christian	Middle Class	Democratic
23	30-34	North - Central	Igede	Master's	Associate	1-5 years	6-10	$25,001-$40,000	Christian	Middle Class	Situational
24	30-34	South-West	Yoruba	Master's	Associate	1-5 years	1-5	$40,001-$55,000	Christian	Middle Class	Democratic
25	35-39	South-East	Ibo	Bachelor	Owner	6-10 years	6-10	Under $25,000	Christian	Middle Class	Democratic
26	35-39	South - South	Oron	Bachelor	Owner	6-10 years	1-5	Under $25,000	Christian	Middle Class	Bureaucratic
27	40-44	North-Central	Ebira	Master's	Associate	1-5 years	1	under $25,000	Christian	Middle Class	Democratic
28	30-34	South-West	Yoruba	Master's	Associate	6-10 years	Over 20 people	$40,001-$55,000	Christian	Middle Class	Situational
29	35-39	North-central	Tiv	Bachelor	Management	6-10 years	6-10	Under $25,000	Christian	Middle Class	Situational
30	45 and Over	South-East	Ibo	Doctorate	Associate	15-20 years	1	Over $55,001	Christian	Upper Class	Transformational

SURVEY QUESTIONNAIRE

Leadership Culture Styles Assessment

The following questions are asked to explore the participant's perspective of how culture and religion affects leadership styles of women and how women view and use of power in Nigeria.

Pre-requisite for participating in this proposed research study are as follows: (a) serve as a leader in an organization or business (b) manage a minimum of one person, (c) possess a minimum of one year of leadership, work or business experience, and (d) experience issues with culture and leadership.

The first part of the survey contains a set of 10 demographic questions to be used in determining the family, economic, and religious backgrounds of women leaders who are in positions of power.

The second part of the survey consists of 15 questions that will be used in determining how women view and use positions of power to lead in their respective 21st century organizations amidst the national and societal culture and religious practices in Nigeria.

DEMOGRAPHIC QUESTIONS

Name: Date:
Organization or Business:

Email address:

Please check the one that applies to you where applicable by placing an X next to the selection:

1.   Please select your age group.

❑ 30 - 34   ❑ 35 - 39   ❑ 40 – 44   ❑ 45 and over

2.   What Nigerian (a) region or zone and (b) local government are your from?

❑ East   ❑ North   ❑ South   ❑ West   ❑ Zone_____

3.   What is your ethnic group? _____

4. Please indicate your highest education level?

❑ Associate's ❑ Bachelor's ❑ Master's ❑ Doctorate ❑ Other__

5. What is your current position within your organization?

❑ Management ❑ Executive ❑ Partner ❑ Owner ❑ Other _____

6. How long have you held your leadership position?

❑ 1 - 5 years ❑ 6-10 years ❑ 7-14 years ❑ 15-20 years ❑ over 20 years

7. How many people are you responsible for managing?

❑ 1 – 5 ❑ 6 - 10 ❑ 7 - 14 ❑ 15 - 20 ❑ over 20 people

8. What is your annual salary range in USD?

❑ Under $25,000 ❑ $25,001-$40,000 ❑ $40,001-$55,000 ❑ over $55,001

9. What is your religious background? Check one or all that applies:

❑ Christian ❑ Muslim ❑ African Traditional Religion (ATR) ❑ Other

10. How would you describe your family background? Check the one that applies:

❑ Very rich – high upper class

❑ Well to do – upper class

❑ Comfortable - Middle class

❑ Poor – Just managing - low middle class

❑ Very poor – hard to cope

This concludes the demographic questions. You may now proceed to filling out the open-ended questions on the next page. Please take your time in writing down the responses. Feel free to express yourself and write as much as you wish. You may use additional space if needed. Your opinion is highly valued and appreciated. Thank you.

Leadership Culture Styles Assessment

1. Thinking about your leadership experience, what would you describe as obstacles you have encountered as a Generation X woman between the ages of 30 to 45 and leading people or managing an organization in the 21st century?

2. What is your view of power as a woman in a leadership position?

3. How do your subordinates (both men and women) treat you as a woman in a position of power belonging to the Generation X group?

4. Describe an asset of the use of your power within your organization or business.

5. Describe the power you possess as a woman belonging to the Generation X group.

6. Describe your view on the role of both the national and family culture on women's leadership (keeping in mind those belonging to the Generation X group).

7. Do you consider your cultural values when exerting your power in your organization or business? Please kindly explain.

8. What do you believe are the general differences in respect to leadership styles between Generation X women leaders and those of women who precede you based on your experiences and assumptions?

9. In your opinion, how do women of previous generations (i.e. baby boomers) treat you, the Generation X woman in a position of power?

10. How has your educational, economic, and religious backgrounds affected your leadership style and your view of power?

11. How would you define your leadership and decision making style? Check one:

    ❑ Autocratic or Authoritarian: you retain total power to yourself and control employees by making all the decision in the organization (i.e. you do not need feedback from others to make a decision in the organization).

    ❑ Bureaucratic: you conduct everything by the book and follow set organizational rules before making a decision (i.e. everything has to be done by the book).

❑ Democratic: you collaborate with staff and receive their feedback before you make the final decision (i.e. everyone gets the opportunity to provide their input).

❑ Laissez Faire: hands off approach where you provide no leadership and let employees make the decisions (i.e. so far as everyone is doing their job, you provide no leadership).

❑ Situational: you adapt to every situation, task or employee (i.e. you have no set leadership style and your decision changes with every situation within the organization).

❑ Transformational: you lead by example, inspiring mentoring and motivating others (i.e. employees look up to you).

12. Describe your reason(s) for selecting the leadership style above, and how you use the selected leadership style within your organization or business on a day-to-day basis.

13. Describe the challenges you face on a day-to-day basis in exercising your leadership style within your organization.

14. How has societal, national culture or family background affected your leadership style and your view of power?

15. Would you have selected or utilized a different leadership style in exercising your power within your organization other than the one that you have selected above if it meant adhering to a "universal" style of leadership to lead effectively in the 21st century? If so, please kindly explain.

OPEN-ENDED QUESTIONS

The following outline was used by the researcher to gather themes or key words for the open ended section of the research questionnaire. This has been included for those who may wish to conduct a leadership styles and culture assessment survey.

1. Obstacles encountered

2. View of power

3. Treatment subordinates or colleague

4. Asset of the use of your power

5. Power as a Generation X group woman

6. View on role national and family culture

7. Cultural values when exerting power

8. Differences in leadership of previous generation

9. Treatment by previous generation

10. A) Effect of background on leadership style:

      1) Education
      2) Economic
      3) Religion

10. B) Effect of background on view of power

      1) Education
      2) Economic
      3) Religion

11. Leadership and decision-making style?

      a. Autocratic or Authoritarian
      b. Bureaucratic
      c. Democratic
      d. Laissez Faire
      e. Situational
      f. Transformational

12. Reason(s) for selecting:

      A) Leadership style
      B) Day-to-day use of selected leadership style

13. Challenges faced in exercising leadership style.

14. Effect of societal, national culture or family background on:

    A) Leadership style
    B) View of power

15. Would you have selected or utilized a different leadership style in exercising your power within your organization other than the one that you have selected above if it meant adhering to a "universal" style of leadership to lead effectively in the 21st century?

www.ingramcontent.com/pod-product-compliance
Lightning Source LLC
Chambersburg PA
CBHW060534210326
41519CB00014B/3214